B

I SURVIVED

My Name is Yitzkhak

By Isadore Neiman

Recorded and Written by
Dr. Harry A. Butowsky

Harry Butowsky

WORD ASSOCIATION PUBLISHERS

$18.00

ISBN: 978-1-63385-100-9
Library of Congress Control Number: 2015915946

Published by
Word Association Publishers
205 Fifth Avenue
Tarentum, Pennsylvania 15084

www.wordassociation.com
1.800.827.7903

I would like to dedicate this book to the memory
of the following individuals:

Dr. J. Alden Nichols 1919-2014
Professor of History
University of Illinois
Urbana/Champaign, Illinois

Simon J. Denenberg, ESQ. 1934 -2015
Philadelphia, Pennsylvania

Contents

Preface

It is a privilege to present Mr. Isadore Neiman's story. Mr. Neiman was born in 1912 in Czuczewicze, Poland, which was then part of the Russian Empire. He lived in Czuczewicze until June 22, 1941, the beginning of the German invasion of Russia during World War II. From June 22, 1941, until he emigrated to the U.S. in 1951, Mr. Neiman was caught in the winds of war, unable to continue his former life, just trying to survive. During this period, life was hard and cheap, and the fact that Mr. Neiman survived the war is truly remarkable. His story is a personal one. He knew nothing of the larger conflict between Germany and Russia that surrounded him; he was only focused on finding enough bread and milk to survive another day. For four long years, Mr. Neiman used his wits, hard work, and considerable luck to live through the conflict, dodging conscription and certain death on the front lines, arrest by the Soviets, and starvation in a Russian work camp. Most of his family, friends, and acquaintances were not so fortunate. He lost almost everyone in the war.

I first met Mr. Neiman in August 1974 in Long Branch, New Jersey, where he was living with his wife, daughter, son-in law, and new grandson. This was many years after the war, but the events of 1941 to 1945 were still very much with him.

At the time, my wife and I were also living in Long Branch with our newborn son. I had just finished a three-year contract at Monmouth College (now Monmouth University) and was teaching part-time while looking for more permanent employment. The Secretary of Monmouth's History Department knew the Neiman family and thought that since we both had newborn sons we should get together. She introduced us, and I will always remain grateful to her for doing so.

My wife and I would visit with Mrs. Neiman and her daughter, son-in-law, and grandchild every few weeks to talk about our experiences as new parents. Mrs. Neiman was from Russia and taught Russian at the local high school. During our visits, I also met Mr. Neiman, who was friendly but reserved. He kept mostly to himself and did not participate in our group discussions.

I gradually began to get him to talk about his life in Europe and during the war. He was reluctant to do so at first, but after some time he opened up to me. I immediately realized that he had a remarkable story to tell and decided that I should record what he had to say. By the fall of 1974, I began to visit with him once a week with my tape recorder. We would talk for one or two hours, and then I would transcribe the material. This continued for more than a year.

Mr. Neiman spoke fluent English, but many times he could not express himself fully in it, so he would switch to Yiddish, then Russian, and finally to Polish. He was always asking me, "You understand?" After several tries in several languages, I managed to understand.

During the months Mr. Neiman and I talked, he was still worried that the Communists would be interested in his illegal activities during the war and that he or the people he talked about would be arrested and sent to jail. I thought he was somewhat paranoid on this matter, but after I was able to listen to his entire story, I realized that it was this same paranoia that had kept him alive during the war.

Soviet Russia in World War II was unlike any society that can be imagined today. The secret police were every-where, and you could be stopped at any time of the day or night, arrested, and sent to Deep Russia (Siberia) or put into the front ranks of the army. Life for the average person was so difficult that everyone had to lie, cheat, and steal to survive. It was just a way of life. In many ways, it was a lawless society, but people followed moral rules. Mr. Neiman would do what he had to do to survive, but he would never hurt anyone or steal from someone who could not afford to lose the food he was after. During his time in Russia, in spite of great privation, he would share food and resources with those who were less fortunate. Mr. Neiman was not alone in doing this. He witnessed many acts of kindness by ordinary Russians.

In early 1976, I finished the manuscript and gave Mr. Neiman a copy. I visited him, but was not able to go over the manuscript in detail with him or ask the questions I still had. Soon after my last visit with him in 1976, I moved to another area of New Jersey and eventually to Washington, DC, where I worked for the National Park Service for 36 years. I never saw Mr. Neiman again.

From 1976 until 2015, I looked at Mr. Neiman's manuscript from time to time. It was sitting on my bookshelf, and I would take it into my World War II in Europe class at George Mason University to read sections to my students. His story always seemed to entrance my students, who wanted to know more about his life in Russia.

While going though one of my closets earlier this year, my daughter found the tapes I had recorded years earlier. In spite of the decades that had passed, I was able to purchase a new tape machine and listen to them again. As I listened to the tapes, I began to revise the manuscript. Remarkably, I had captured the essence of what Mr. Neiman had to tell me. The main problem was adding the personal and place names. Mr. Neiman did not want to use any personal names that the Russians could use to arrest someone he talked about in his story, so he often used an initial instead, referring to Z_____ rather than

Zelkie, for instance. I have managed to return most of the names to the manuscript, but not all of them. Some people and place names will remain forever unknown.

I was 30 years old at the time I took this oral history, and Mr. Neiman was 62. I always called him Mr. Neiman, and that was what he preferred to be called. Listening to the tapes, there are many questions I wish I could ask Mr. Neiman, but this is not possible. Mr. Neiman died in 2003, and I never saw him again.

The reader may wonder why I do not have more information about Mr. Neiman's first wife, twin sons, parents, and family in this account. I can only say that I did press him for more information about his family, but this was one area he was reluctant to share with me. They were all killed by the Germans in the Holocaust, and the pain was just too obvious. He could not talk about them, and I did not press him to do so.

Finally, let me say that this is Mr. Neiman's story. This is his personal story of survival. All of the people he knew before and during the war are now dead. Their memories are forgotten and lost to the sands of history—except for this recollection. In this book, the lives of Mr. Neiman, his family, and fellow Jews from Czuczewicze, Poland, are preserved and recorded for all to read. In Mr. Neiman's story they are still with us and will live forever.

Harry Butowsky,
Virginia, July 18, 2015

Chronology

Chronology of Isadore Neiman's Life and the Major Events of World War II in Poland and Russia

1912

Historical Context	The village Czuczewicze (now in Belarus-Chuchavichy) is part of the Russian Empire.
Isadore Neiman's Life	Isadore Neiman is born in his grandfather's house in Vautin, nineteen miles from Czuczewicze, in Tsarist Russia.

1914

Historical Context	World War I breaks out. The Russian Tsar orders all Jews to leave their homes and move deeper into Russia.
Isadore Neiman's Life	Mr. Neiman and his family flee to Bobruisk, Russia, and live there for five years.

1917

Historical Context	In October, Vladimir Lenin and the Bolsheviks come to power in the Russian Revolution.

1918

Historical Context	Poland emerges from World War I as an independent state, the Second Polish Republic.

Adolph Hitler will return to Bavaria and will soon form the Nazi party. |
| *Isadore Neiman's Life* | On February 18, Czuczewicze villagers murder Polish Army Colonel Boleslaw Moscicki and suffer the Polish Army's retribution as the Army occupies Czuczewicze. |

1919

Historical Context	Poland fights border wars with Russia, which are collectively referred to as the Polish–Soviet War.

In June 1919, the Treaty of Versailles confirms Poland's independent status. |
| *Isadore Neiman's Life* | In 1919, the Neiman family and other Jewish residents return to Czuczewicze, which is in the territory disputed by the Soviet Union and Poland. |

Russian and Polish soldiers move frequently around Czuczewicze. The border between Russian and Poland is still not determined. Russian soldiers steal food, clothing and horses from Czuczewicze citizens.

1921

Historical Context

On March 18, the Treaty of Riga ends the Polish-Soviet War.

In peacetime, Poland experiences economic growth. One-third of its population is made up of national minorities (Ukrainians, Jews, Belarusians

In peacetime, Poland experiences economic growth.

Isadore Neiman's Life

Mr. Neiman and his family moves from smaller to larger Czuczewicze (Wielkie Czuczewicze).

The Polish Army occupies Czuczewicze and will remain there for several years. The army brings peace and stability to the area and is welcome by the Jewish population

1922	
Historical Context	Poland's frontiers are settled.
1923	
Historical Context	Poland's borders are internationally recognized. It is a democratic, but politically-chaotic nation.
1926	
Historical Context	In May, Jozef Pilsudski seizes power and ends Polish democracy.
Isadore Neiman's Life	Polish soldiers who had been living with the village's farmers leave Czuczewicze.
1928	
Historical Context	Adolph Hitler is expanding the reach of the Nazi Party from Bavaria to the whole of Germany.
Isadore Neiman's Life	Mr. Neiman's grandfather passes away. Mr. Neiman works for his father.
1932–35	
Historical Context	In January 1933, Hitler and the Nazi Party come to power in Germany. Attacks on German Jews intensify. Jewish businesses are boycotted, and Jews are attacked on the streets. Many German Jews attempt to flee, but most nations,

including the United States, close their doors to Jewish emigration.

The Nuremberg Laws are introduced on September 15, 1935, in Germany, declaring that only those of German or related blood are eligible to be Reich citizens. All others are classed as state subjects without citizenship rights.

Isadore Neiman's Life

Due to universal conscription laws in Poland, Mr. Neiman serves in the Polish Army in a cavalry unit for the first time. He is stationed near the German border.

Mr. Neiman and the Jews of Czuczewicze hear about Hitler but are not really aware of his hatred of the Jews. The Jewish population of Czuczewice has almost no knowledge of the outside world.

1937

Historical Context

On November 5, Hitler holds a secret meeting and states his plans for acquiring Lebensraum, or "living space," for the German people.

Isadore Neiman's Life

Mr. Neiman serves one required month in the Polish Army.

1939

Historical Context

In August, Germany and Russia secretly agree to partition Poland.

On September 1, Germany invades Poland. They practice total war, focusing their attacks on both military and civilian targets.

On September 28, Warsaw falls to the German army.

On October 5, the Polish military's resistance ends.

Germany and Russia divide Poland: Germany takes the west, and Russia takes the eastern portions.

Isadore Neiman's Life

In the summer, Mr. Neiman's brother is called up for military service. Resistance to German invasion ends before Mr. Neiman is called up.

Czuczewicze (in eastern Poland) comes under Soviet control.

Communist prisoners are released and put in charge of Polish cities and towns.

1939-40

Historical Context

The Soviet Union's NKVD (People's Commissariat of Internal Affairs) arrest 109,000 Polish citizens.

Polish Jews fleeing from German-occupied Poland are rounded up and deported into Russia. Those Jews who return to the German-occupied areas of Poland later die in the Holocaust.

Isadore Neiman's Life

Mr. Neiman and his fellow citizens of Czuczewicze hear terrible stories from Jews and Poles fleeing German-controlled western Poland. Many Polish Jews from German occupied Poland take refuge in Czuczewicze and live with Jewish families.

Mr. Neiman works as a butcher until 1941.

Mr. Neiman marries his first wife.

1940

Historical Context

On March 5, Polish Officers who had been Russian prisoners are executed during the Katyn Massacre.

Isadore Neiman's Life

Mr. Neiman's twin sons are born.

The Russians put up posters around Czuczewicze to trick Jewish refugees from German-occupied land into signing up on lists to return home (they are actually sent to deeper into Russia).

1941

Historical Context

On June 22, Germany invades the Soviet Union in Operation Barbarossa.

Soviet authorities announce that all young men must report for military duty.

In August, Franklin Roosevelt and Winston Churchill meet to sign the Atlantic Charter and agree that when the United States comes into the war Germany will be the prime adversary to be defeated

The German Army advances in the USSR fight until December, when the Russians stop the Germans in the freezing snows of Moscow and force the Germans to retreat.

On December 7, Japan bombs Pearl Harbor, bringing the U.S. into the war. Hitler declares war on America on December 11, 1941.

On Christmas Day 1941, 3,700 Russian civilians starve to death in the siege of Leningrad.

By December 1941 the Russian army has lost more than 2 million men in combat.

Isadore Neiman's Life

In May, Mr. Neiman is accused by the Russian government of cheating the government when buying cows. He is told he will have to stand trial for this offense

The night of June 21-22, the Czuczewicze villagers know war has begun.

On June 22, Mr. Neiman and all other young men in the village must join the Russian army. They go first to Luninets, then Grodno.

On June 27, the Germans occupy Czuczewicze and most citizens flee. Mr. Neiman's paternal uncle is killed.

During June and July, the Germans round up all of the remaining Jewish men in Czuczewicze and shoot them.

Throughout the summer, Mr. Neiman travels with the Russian Army, moving (on foot and on trains) toward Deep Russia to avoid Germans at the front. The Army is bombed by German planes while traveling. He sees his first war dead during this trip.

On November 1, Mr. Neiman is in Tula, near Moscow, still walking away from the front with Russian officers. He works loading ammunition onto trains for Russians to use in December during the Battle of Moscow.

1942

Historical Context

At the Wannsee Conference in January 1942, the Deputy Chief of the SS, Reinhard Heydrich, convenes a meeting of top German military and political officials to decide the fate of all the Jews in German-occupied lands. Plans are drawn up for the complete extermination of all the Jews of Europe.

Ninety percent of Poland's Jewish population of 3.5 million are murdered in concentration camps or during mass killings during the Holocaust. The Germans use poison gas, which they determined was the most effective means of executing so many people.

Isadore Neiman's Life

In February, Mr. Neiman joins the Polish Army again. He serves in it for three months, then leaves. While all the soldiers are Polish the Officers are Russian.

On May 1, Mr. Neiman narrowly escapes being murdered by a Ukrainian criminal.

In June, Mr. Neiman is sick with malaria.

From July 1942 to July 1943, Mr. Neiman works for Alexi (the Director) hauling goods from a train station.

In August 1942 all of the remaining Jews living in Czuczewicze, including Mr. Neiman's mother, wife, and twin sons, are taken to Auschwitz and gassed.

1943

Historical Context

The Germans are defeated at Stalingrad in January and again at the Battle of Kursk in July. The Russian Army takes the initiative against the Germans.

Germany is on the defensive, and most military leaders know that the war is lost. Adolph Eichmann, who is in charge of the extermination of the Jews of Europe, speeds up the killing machinery. Eichmann enlists all of the manpower and transportation resources he can command to kill the remaining Jews still living in Europe.

Isadore Neiman's Life

While in Russia Mr. Neiman's brother is almost caught illegally slaughtering a cow.

In July, all of Mr. Neiman's belongings are stolen during a train ride when he leaves the Director to join the Polish Army again. He later decides not to join.

Mr. Neiman is arrested by the NKVD for traveling without papers. He is sent to a Russian work camp as a prisoner.

From July 1943 to October 1944, Mr. Neiman is held captive in a Russian work camp. Life is very difficult there. Food rations are minimal.

1944

Historical Context

German forces retreat from the USSR, murdering Jews and prisoners and burning towns along the way.

On June 6, the American, British, and Canadian forces invade France in Operation Overlord

Germany is now fighting a major war on two fronts.

In July 1944, German Army Colonel Klaus von Stauffenberg attempts to kill Hitler but is not successful. Hitler will ultimately kill 5,000 Germans in revenge for this failed plot.

On July 24, the first German concentration camp is discovered in Poland by the Russian army. Reports are immediately sent out to the British and Americans, who discount them.

In December, the German Army launches its last major offensive in the West, The Battle of the Bulge. The German offensive fails, and the final collapse of Germany begins.

Isadore Neiman's Life

In October, Mr. Neiman escapes the work camp while being moved by train. He goes to Eulenburg to join his cousin at another collective.

During the autumn, Mr. Neiman works in a slaughterhouse in Eulenburg.

During the winter, Mr. Neiman works for a blacksmith in a collective.

1945

Historical Context

On April 30, the Russians surround Berlin, and Hitler kills himself rather than be taken prisoner.

On May 7, Germany surrenders.

Victory Day in the USSR happens on May 9.

The United Nations is established in June.

On May 14, Mr. Neiman learns that the war is over.

Mr. Neiman realizes that most of his family is dead, killed by the Germans. He is determined not to return to Poland. He hears that many Polish Jews who returned to their homes have been killed by Poles.

During the spring and summer, Mr. Neiman works as a farmhand and shepherd at a collective.

In mid July, Mr. Neiman is taken to the forest to cut wood. He works in a warehouse and on a sewer.

In the autumn, Mr. Neiman meets and marries his second wife, a Russian citizen.

1946

The new government of Poland is Communist and loyal to Russia.

Tensions between the Russians and the English and Americans are increasing. Winston Churchill visits the United States and gives the famous speech in which he announces the beginning of the Cold War and coins the term "Iron Curtain."

In May, Mr. Neiman and his wife leave Russia on a cargo train going to Poland. Mr. Neiman is determined not to return to Poland. His family is dead, and his life there is over. He is committed to making a new life for himself and his wife in the West.

During the train ride, Mr. Neiman and his wife listen to Ukrainian passengers brag about killing Jews during the war.

In June, Mr. Neiman and his wife live in a refugee camp in former German-occupied Poland, then in a Kibbutz run by Hagana.

In the summer, Mr. Neiman and his wife are smuggled into Czechoslovakia, then onto a train to an Austrian refugee camp.

1947

Historical Context

On November 29, the United Nations General Assembly recommends the adoption and implementation of the Partition Plan for Mandatory Palestine. This Plan creates the State of Israel, which officially is born at midnight on May 14, 1948. Its Arab neighbors immediately launch an invasion, sparking a conflict that continues today.

Isadore Neiman's Life

On January 9, Mr. Neiman's daughter is born in an Austrian refugee camp.

Mr. Neiman works selling kosher meat in the Austrian camp. Strict rationing makes his activity illegal, but Mr. Neiman continues.

Mr. Neiman waits for the paperwork he will need to travel to America with his wife and daughter.

1950

Historical Context

In June, the Korean War begins.

Isadore Neiman's Life

HIAS (Hebrew Immigrant Aid Society) agrees to help the Neimans emigrate to the U.S.

1951

Isadore Neiman's Life

The Neimans arrive in the U.S. Mr. Neiman will find a job in Trenton, New Jersey, working in an air conditioner factory, and he will later move to Long Branch, New Jersey, where he will work as a kosher butcher.

In June 1974, Mr. Neiman's grandson is born, and my wife and I meet him and his family.

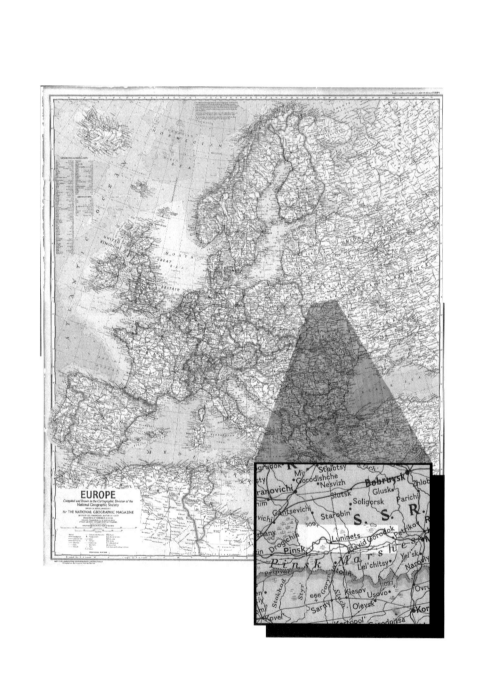

EUROPE
Compiled and Drawn in the Cartographic Division of the
National Geographic Society
for THE NATIONAL GEOGRAPHIC MAGAZINE

chapter one

My Early Life in Poland

My name is Isadore Neiman. In Jewish [Yiddish], my name is Yitzkhak. I was born in 1912 in Russia—during the time of the Tsars [the pre-Soviet era]—in my mother's village of Vautin,[1] which was nineteen miles distant from my village of Czuczewicze. My mother and father were cousins. Many Jews married distant relations. We never traveled very far from the village, and it was difficult to meet someone who was not a friend or a distant relative. It was also dangerous to travel too far from home. Many people would rob and kill Jews if they had a chance to do so. It was much safer to stay home where we knew our neighbors and trusted them.

I was born in my maternal grandfather's house in Vautin. My grandfather was a blacksmith. He was a very

---

1   Editor's Note: Throughout this narrative, I have transcribed the names in Mr. Neiman's story to the best of my ability. Some are doubtless misspelled, as I was unable to locate proper spellings during my research, and some are omitted because Mr. Neiman did not want them identified. For names of people and locations that are intelligible in the recording or that Mr. Neiman wished to keep to himself, I have used only their first letter.

handy person and could make almost anything with his hands. Every village needed a blacksmith to fix things. We made everything by hand because there were no factories. My grandfather could build a whole wagon from just the lumber and metal scraps he had in his shop. He could make horseshoes and horse nails by hand. Every horse needed twenty-four nails and four horseshoes, so there was always plenty of work for my grandfather. I learned how to be a blacksmith from him and my father. It was a good way to make a living.

I was the oldest of four children. I had two brothers and one sister. One brother was in the Russian Army and disappeared. We never knew what happened to him. My sister was killed by the Germans in 1942, and my other brother now lives in Israel.

Most of the people living in the villages where I grew up were White Russians [Belarusians]. They were all farmers. The Russian farmers always needed a blacksmith to work for them, so they would get together to encourage one to settle in their village. They gave my grandfather a house to live in with a large garden. Most of the houses in our village had only one large room. Only rich villagers had houses with more than one room. My grandfather also had some cows that the village gave him. The farmers had no money and would pay my grandfather in food, which was usually potatoes.

My paternal grandfather was also a blacksmith. He lived in the village of Czuczewicze where I lived as a boy.

There were two villages called Czuczewicze, and we lived in the larger Czuczewicze.[2] I remember in my village was a little store, which we called a Kretchme. It was owned by a Jewish family and had everything that the farmers needed to buy. The Kretchme sold soap, kerosene, cloth, nails, and sugar. The Kretchme also served as a local meeting hall for the farmers. The farmers would come to the Kretchme and buy some vodka and tobacco and could smoke and drink for the night. It was a place they could go and be alone for a while. They could also meet with one another and play cards and talk and have a good time.

There were only a few Jews in every village. In my village of Czuczewicze we had only twenty Jewish families and about three hundred fifty Russian families. The Jews were not farmers. During the time of the Tsars, they were not allowed to own any land. After the First World War, they could legally own land, but the farmers would never sell them any land. The farmers only wanted to buy land and not sell it. The Jews earned their living by buying and selling. They were all traders or craftsmen.

My uncle lived across the street from my house. He was a businessman. He had two daughters who lived and two sons who died. My paternal grandmother lived in little Czuczewicze about two kilometers from us. After my grandfather died in 1929, she came to my village and lived with my uncle. She was over seventy at the time and knew everyone in the village. She had a name for all the

---

2   Editor's Note: Now known as Wielkie Czuczewicze, Belarus.

farmers and was a real gossip. Soon even the farmers were using her names. One farmer was The Pit, while another was The Bear, and a third was The Fox. The rest of my relatives lived in Vautin and Luninets, which were not far from us.

The farmers tried to make everything for themselves, but they couldn't always do this and had to buy from the Jews in the village. That was how the Jews earned a living: they sold goods to the farmers. Everyone worked hard in the village, and life was good. We were poor by modern standards, but we didn't know it. We really did not know anything about what was happening in the world beyond our local village. We all worked hard and had a good life. Everything was nice and quiet.

There were two blacksmiths in my village for a time. My grandfather was there first, and most of the farmers came to him. The other blacksmith had a hard time and eventually had to leave. There was not enough work for two men.

My father helped his father in the shop when there was a lot of work to do. He was also very good with his hands. He did not become a blacksmith because there was not enough work for two men in the village, so he was a general handyman and part-time trader. He would help the farmers build their houses. They would do the rough work, and he would finish with the detailed work. He would put in the windows and the doors. It was skilled work, and he had to know just what to do. My father also built ovens for the homes. These were brick ovens, which he built on a wooden foundation high above the ground. In winter, the farmers would let the chickens and pigs stay under the ovens to keep warm. Some people in the village had sewing machines, and my father would fix them also. He fixed everything for the village. No one ever threw anything out if it could be fixed or salvaged. There was very little waste in the village. We were too poor for that.

My father was the oldest boy in his family. He had two brothers: one brother left the village in 1905 and went to America, where he worked for many years in a slaughterhouse in Hartford, Connecticut. He died in 1920 as a result of an accident at work. We never really heard too much about him. My father's other brother lived in Czuczewicze until the Second World War started. He was killed by the Germans in 1941 when they came to the village.

My grandmother lived with us, and she would help my mother around the house. My mother would get up at five in the morning to make the fire. We had no coal and had to make the fire out of wood, which we took from the forest. The wood was not free. We had to pay a fee for it to a rich Polish nobleman who lived in Paris and who owned the forest. We cut the wood from the forest during the winter. It was hard work, but it had to be done. We had little furniture in our house. It was just a plain house with a few beds, a table, and chairs.

My father would get up after my mother and give hay to the cows and take care of the other animals. My mother would then begin to cook potatoes for breakfast. Sometimes she would also make bread and give us milk for breakfast. For lunch we had more potatoes, usually in a soup with a piece of cabbage. We ate a lot of potatoes because they were cheap. They were also very good, and I could eat potatoes all day even now. We never became tired of them. After breakfast, my mother would milk the cow and put the milk in large pots that were used just for milk. She would let the milk stand for two days and get sour cream. If the milk was very rich, the sour cream would be three fingers deep; if not, then it was two fingers deep. She also made butter from the milk. We children always liked the milk best when it came right from the cow. It was warm and delicious. We had four cows at home and had enough milk.

My mother would then make the beds. There were only three beds in the house. My father and mother each had a bed and my sister had a bed. My two brothers and I slept on wooden benches on which we put fresh hay for a mattress. If it was cold outside, we covered up with blankets and our coats. The bench was always very comfortable, and I always slept very well. The house had just one large room with a small partition where my parents slept.

My mother did all the washing by hand. She would wash once a week and put all the clothes in large wooden tubs and put in hot water from the oven. It was very hard work, and sometimes my mother had a farmer's girl to help her. We would pay her with five pounds of salt. She would rinse the clothes in a nearby stream.

We children would go to school every morning. The Jewish families in the village always hired a teacher to teach us Hebrew and the Bible. Boys and girls both went to school. We learned all about the great Jewish teachers and the Talmud, and we had to memorize the opinions of the great Jewish philosophers. We would also learn to read in Russian. It was considered enough for a girl to read and write, but boys were expected to learn more. A boy always had to have as much education as possible. He might even go to the yeshiva to study, though this was very difficult for most families to do. Only a very few boys could go to town to study at the yeshiva. Most families couldn't afford the cost. Jewish boys in town always stayed with Jewish families. They would live with one family for a week and then with another family. The whole community had to work together to help the students. That was how it was done; everyone in the Jewish community contributed a little to keep the yeshiva open. The actual amount of money needed to keep a boy in the yeshiva was not great, but many families had nothing at all and needed their sons home to work for the family. It was a great honor to have a son who became a Rabbi or perhaps a Shochet (a man who performs ritual slaughter of cattle). I stopped going to school at fifteen. That was enough, and I had to work.

I never went to the yeshiva. My teacher came to our village and was hired for a specific period of time. It usually cost about two dollars in American money to send a child to school. We studied from eight in the morning to noon. We had one hour for lunch, and then we worked from one to six. The teacher stayed with all the Jewish families in the village. He spent a few days with every family. I remember when he stayed with my family. He would eat dinner with us and then do his work by the fire. At night, he would sleep with the cows. I always had homework to do at night. I usually worked on my Jewish studies first and then did my Russian and later Polish. (I saw my teacher in Russia after the war began. He survived the war and came to New York City, where he is now living.)

After the First World War, when we became part of Poland, the government set up public schools in the village for all the children. Everyone had to go. The Jews were happy and wanted to go to the Polish school, but the Russians were indifferent to it. They tried to avoid the school. Even then I still had to study my Jewish subjects at night.

My family usually had dinner at six in the evening. We had potatoes and milk, and on rare occasions some herring. I loved to eat that food and never became tired of the potatoes. We had no baths then and didn't seem to need them. We just washed ourselves with a cloth and that was that. We were clean without taking baths. By eight or nine, soon after dark, we were always in bed. Kerosene was expensive to burn, so we went to sleep.

Sometimes I would take our horse out into the woods with the other boys from the village. I would put a tie on his feet so he couldn't walk far while he grazed on the fresh grass. We would then make a fire and cook potatoes in the fire. This was good for the horse because he had fresh grass and got away from the flies and mosquitoes. (The insects were terrible in the summer and bothered both animals and people greatly. They were so thick that they would cover the entire back of a horse.) I really enjoyed those times. We had good food and fresh air and could talk the entire night. We had to tie the feet of the horse so he would eat well. If we let the horse wander, he would walk around a lot and not get enough to eat. The potatoes we had to eat from the fire were the best I ever had in my entire life. The smell of the cooking potatoes and the clean fresh air of the forest always made us hungry. It was a good time.

We had one main street and three or four cross streets. All the houses in the village were located close to each other. A farmer never had to walk more than one or two kilometers to get to his fields. The farmers had only a few acres, and the farms were all small by American standards. Sometimes a farmer would buy land in the woods from the noble and have to clear it. That was always very hard work because there were a lot of tree stumps to pull from the ground. There was never enough land for the farmers. If they had many sons, the land was divided and then there was even less. They always wanted to buy more land. No farmer ever sold land if he could help it.

We knew very little about what was happening outside of the village. We had no radio or television. Once a month we would get a Jewish paper from Warsaw, and the whole village would read it. Sometimes we heard news from travelers who passed through our village. We were interested in the world outside of the village, but had a hard time finding out about it. We just did not know much about life outside of our village.

The farmers would sometimes drink at night and fight when they were drunk. Sometimes they would lose their tempers completely and someone would be hurt or even killed. They would buy a bottle of vodka and go into their homes and sit and drink and eat salt pork. Many times the young boys of the village would fight over the village girls.

There was very little crime in the village. Everyone knew everyone else. The police knew who all the troublemakers were. I remember once someone broke into a neighbor's house and stole his alarm clock. The next day the police came to the village thief and began to search around in his barn. Sure enough they found the clock in his hay loft. The clock started to ring while they were looking for it. The thief got four months in the jail in the city. It was hard to go to jail because the cells were very small, and the police made you stay in the cell all the time. The police knew who all the troublemakers were and could usually solve any crime quickly. The farmers would usually fight at weddings and holidays.

The farmers always married local girls. I remember one farmer who worked hard and had a good farm with no children or family. When he became old, he found it hard to work the farm. He found a local boy and girl and told them if they got married and came to live with him, he would eventually give them his farm. It was a good deal for that boy. He was my neighbor and had a good reputation in the village. The farmer had known him since he was a baby and was sure of him. He took care of the old man, and he and his wife eventually got the farm. Everyone was happy.

We never had any money. The only important thing was to have enough food to eat and a place to sleep and clothing to wear. There was no doctor in the village. If you were sick, you just went to bed until you were better. If you were really ill, you could go to the city of Luninets where there was a doctor. That doctor also pulled teeth.

Every Sabbath, we all went to pray in the synagogue, and every week we met in a different house to pray. We couldn't afford to build a regular synagogue. There were thirty Jewish families in the village, so it seemed as if there was always a crowd at Sabbath services. We prayed from eight in the morning to noon. We never worked on Saturday. We also prayed every Friday night. After Friday night services, we would eat supper and then go to bed.

We had shoes only for Sabbath services, and we never wore shoes in the village. Only in winter would we wear heavy boots. When a boy had his Bar Mitzvah, his parents would come to the shul [synagogue] and bring a bottle of vodka. The boy would go to the Torah and say his part, and the parents would give everyone a little drink. When there was a marriage, all the Jewish families would come to the house to celebrate. We would play music and dance the entire night. The next morning we would all go to work. Even the newly-married couple had to go to work. There was no vacation. We worked all of the time.

We had a good life in the village. We were poor in material wealth, but rich with other goods. It was a happy life, and I still miss it.

Typical House in Luninets, Belarus today

Rural Road in the Woods at Czuczewicze, Belarus

Chapter Two

The Colonel

The First World War started in August 1914, and the Tsar ordered all of the Jews to leave their homes. We were given two days to pack up and leave our village. The Jews put everything they could onto their wagons and left. We moved to Bobruisk, which was located about two hundred kilometers east of Czuczewicze, deep in Russia. Many Jewish families had to move even deeper into Russia. The farmers took everything the Jews left behind. They even moved into some of the empty houses.

We lived in Deep Russia for four years. After the Russian Revolution and the end of the war, the Jews began to go back to their homes. Conditions were very hard for everyone after the war. My father took any type of work that he could find to support his family. After the war, there was no real government, and many Jews were killed by robbers while trying to return to their homes. Still, we wanted to go home to our village. It was where we belonged. There was no government to tell us not to go home, so in 1919, my family returned to Czuczewicze.

My grandfather was the first member of my family to return to our village. When he got back, he found that his house had been destroyed in the war. Only the walls and roof were left. All the doors and windows were missing. The village still needed my grandfather because he was a blacksmith, so they decided he could have my father's house. They told the farmer who was living there that he would have to move. My grandfather lived there alone for most of the year. The rest of my family stayed in Deep Russia to wait for his word to return. We came back to the village before the end of the year and rented another house because my father didn't want to put his father out. Our new house was small and not nearly large enough, but it had a small plot of land around it. We soon had some cows and chickens, and life was back to normal. My grandfather and my uncle Moishe (Moses) fixed up my grandfather's old house, and my uncle moved in with his family.

My father did everything he could to make a living and provide food for his children. Within a short time, the Jewish families in the village had hired a teacher, and, as the oldest child, I was back in school. By 1921, we had moved from small Czuczewicze to large Czuczewicze, about two kilometers away. We moved there because the teacher was there, and it was easier for us to go to school in the larger village.

During this time, conditions were still uncertain in our village. We saw many armies pass through the area, both Russian and Polish. Every few weeks we were occupied by a different army. They were fighting for control of the land. Before the war, we were part of Russia, but after the war the Polish government claimed us. The Polish Army finally drove the Russians out, and we became part of Poland. We still lived very close to the Russian border, and sometimes Russian soldiers would cross the border to steal from us.

The soldiers took everything from us. They couldn't help it. They were always hungry and received nothing from their government. It was not like the United States, where the government gives its soldiers everything they need. They had to find their own food. They would come right into our house and ask for food. They took anything they could eat. The farmers had cows, chickens, fruits, vegetables, and potatoes. The soldiers took the food and ate it right there. They would kill a chicken and cook it right in your front yard. Many people took their food and valuables and hid in the woods when the soldiers came. We were familiar with the woods and knew the soldiers could never find us there. The trees were thick as grass, and it was easy to hide.

We had to be very careful to hide our horses from the army. The army always needed good horses. If some soldiers saw you on the road with a horse, they might take it away from you. They might also draft you into the army for a few days with your horse and force you to drive fifty or one hundred kilometers before they would let you go. It was best to hide in the woods and avoid the soldiers. The Polish Army treated us better than the Russians, but it was still a dangerous time for the Jews. Many Jews were found dead on the road, and no one knew who was responsible. Only after the Polish Army drove out the Russians did our lives improve.

The Jews didn't care who won the war as long as there was peace and some kind of government. We wanted law and order and security for our lives. We wanted the fighting to end. The war was terrible. I remember this time very well. I was a young boy then, and it all seemed very exciting to me. When the soldiers came, my family fled to the woods, where we lived under the stump of a large fallen tree. I remember going back to the village one day and finding the door of our house knocked open. On the table was our large family Bible which the soldiers used to cut up some chickens. They used the pages from the Bible to clean their knives, and there was chicken blood all over them. They didn't know it was a Bible when they used it; they just needed the paper to cut the chickens. They didn't mean any harm.

One day I was walking with my father when we saw two soldiers on horses outside of our village. They were Russians and asked my father where the Polish Army was located. My father didn't know. He said he had been in the woods for many days and had heard nothing about the Polish Army. They let us go, and we went our way.

By 1921, the Polish government firmly established its authority in our area, and living conditions became much better. There was no more robbery and everything went back to normal. For a few years the government sent some Polish soldiers to live in our village. They stayed with the farmers, but by 1926 they left.

⚒ ⚒

About four months before we returned to Czuczewicze in 1919, an interesting event happened in the village. A Polish colonel and two soldiers came to the village from Warsaw.[3] They were making maps for the Polish government. In the woods surrounding our village were many watchmen who guarded the woods from poachers. The watchmen worked for the Polish nobleman, who lived in Paris. He was a rich and important man whom we heard about but never saw. There were many products in the woods that the villagers needed, and it was necessary to guard the woods to prevent any stealing. The watchmen had good jobs because they could take bribes from the villages and steal from the woods themselves in addition to their salary from the noble. Everyone wanted to be a watchman.

3   Editor's Note: Colonel Boleslaw Moscicki, Lieutenant Maximilian Łebkowski, and Sergeant Boleslaw Mroziński.

The watchman lived about twelve kilometers from our village, and his name was Gonshav. He lived in a large cabin in the woods with his wife and two girls and one son. In March 1919, the Polish colonel and the two soldiers came to his cabin and asked if they could spend the night. Gonshav let them in his house and gave them supper. He talked to them and found out what their business was. He also noticed the jewelry of the colonel and his expensive clothes. The colonel asked Gonshav the directions to the town of Byaroza, which was about five kilometers away. Gonshav told him the directions, and then the soldiers all went to sleep. Later that night, Gonshav ran to our village and told his friends about the colonel who was staying at his house. Gonshav's friends from the village got dressed and went into the woods to wait for the colonel. They knew he would come because Gonshav had given them the directions. They wanted to kill the colonel and rob him.

They waited in the woods that morning for the colonel and shot him as soon as they saw him.[4] The two soldiers were not hurt. They robbed the colonel of his money and jewelry and buried him in a shallow grave in the woods. Before they buried him, they cut off his fingers to get his rings. They put leaves over his grave and

---

4   Editor's Note: This incident took place on February 18, 1918. A monument to the Colonel is located in the forest southeast of Deniskowicz near Czuczewicze in Belarus. According to the text of the monument, the Colonel died while fighting the Bolsheviks, but Mr. Neiman's story indicates that this was not the case. Information about the monument may be found at http://www.rowery.olsztyn.pl/wiki/miejsca/1914/bialorus/brzeski/uroczysko_dub.

took the two soldiers back to the village. The soldiers were scared and didn't know what was going to happen to them. They had to walk twelve kilometers to get to the village and were all tired by the time they got there. The two soldiers were taken to the city hall where they were questioned by the villagers and beaten. One man, named Linchuk, beat the soldiers without mercy. He hit them on the face, and they thought for sure they were going to be killed. But the villagers decided to let them go, and the soldiers walked to Luninets where they took a train back to Warsaw. It was about 700 kilometers and took them several days to get back to Warsaw, where they reported the incident to the Polish Army.

For the next few weeks everything was quiet in the village. The incident with the colonel was forgotten. Not many people were even aware of the killing. One month later, the Polish Army came to the village. They came to punish the villagers who killed the colonel and beat the soldiers. They went first to the house of the watchman, Gonshav, and they forced him to go with them to the village. It was late at night, and they wanted to know exactly who was responsible for the killing. Gonshav had no choice. He had to help them. They told him that if he cooperated they would not kill him. He took them to the village, and they went from house to house and rounded up the men who were responsible. Gonshav also showed them the building where the village government was located and where the two soldiers were beaten.

The Army then collected all the men in the village from the age of seventeen to seventy and took them to the courtyard of the building where the village government was found. They visited every house except for the houses of the Jews, who they decided had nothing to do with the killing of the colonel. Only one villager who had helped beat the soldiers managed to escape. The five men who were responsible for the actual killing of the colonel were all caught.

In the backyard, the soldiers found a large wooden bench and took the men one by one and put them over the bench, lowered their pants and beat their backsides with sticks until there was blood. Every man in the village from the age of 17 to 70 was beaten. Some people couldn't sit for months. There were no doctors or medicine to help with the sores.

The five men who killed the colonel were also beaten, and then the soldiers cut out their eyes with their bayonets. Their names were Nicholai, Basel, Bisco, Shakau and Linchuk. They did this all in front of their families. The soldiers then told the families to prepare coffins for the men. By the time the families brought the coffins to the City Hall, the whole village was crying. There was a Polish priest with the troops. When the soldiers wanted to burn the village, the people ran to the priest and asked him to help save the village. The villagers were all crying like babies, and they told the priest that they didn't know anything about the killing of the colonel and were not responsible for his death. The priest persuaded the soldiers to spare the village and just punish the criminals who were directly responsible for the killing.

The condemned men were put in wagons and driven to the cemetery. Each man rode in one wagon with his family. The whole village followed the wagons. Everyone was crying. The soldiers stood the men up in a line at the rear of the cemetery and shot each one in the head with a single bullet. One man was wearing a large fur coat and the bullet lodged in the coat. While the other men were still, he was still thrashing around on the ground. They had to shoot him again before he was quiet.

Then the soldiers took the chief of the village to Warsaw. They returned to the village a few days later and took him into the woods and hanged him. He did not participate in the killings but had allowed the beating of the soldiers in the city hall. The villagers found him a few days later still hanging from a tree. They buried him next to the other five men. I do not know what happened to Gonshav. He just disappeared, and I think he just ran away.

The soldiers then went to the grave of the colonel, dug up his body and put it in a fine casket, and took him back to Warsaw, where he had a magnificent funeral. This all happened in 1919. When my family returned to the village four months later, we heard all about the incident. The villagers remained very much afraid of the Polish Army for many years and were careful to always be on their best behavior. There was no trouble after that time.

The government established tight control over the village. Even though the people were White Russians and the government Polish, there were no problems. They learned their lesson in 1919 with the colonel and did not cause any trouble after that incident.

The dead men were all buried next to each other in the cemetery. They all left wives and children. One of the men, Linchuk, was married only one week when he was killed. Ten years later, the Polish government erected a big monument to the colonel in the woods. It was made of white marble and was surrounded by a heavy metal chain. Many people from Warsaw came to see the monument dedicated. Many Jews went too, but no one from the village was there.

The Jews were happy to see the government take control. We could now make a living. Everything was now quiet, and the Polish Army was in the area in case of any trouble. Eventually the army moved closer to the Russian border, but we had no trouble. Everything was quiet. The villagers had learned their lesson.

Monument to Colonel Boleslaw Moscicki murdered in
Czuczewicze, Poland in 1919. Now located in Belarus.

Colonel Boleslaw Moscicki of the Polish Army in 1919

Chapter Three

Army Life

Many people came to our village in the winter to work in the nearby woods. They processed wood products for the nobleman who owned the woods. As a result of this, by the end of winter there was a lot of material in the village that was valuable to the Russians. The workers would give my mother flour, and she would bake bread for them and keep some of the bread for payment. That was how we supported ourselves for a time.

My family lived twenty miles from the Russian [Belarus] border in 1920. In that year, a group of Russian soldiers came to our village, because they wanted to steal everything they could from us. The soldiers came to our village at two in the afternoon one day. There were four Polish policemen stationed in our village at that time. The soldiers surrounded the police station and cut the telephone wire. One man held a gun on the police and told them not to move. They took all the wood products and horses that belonged to the nobleman who owned the woods and robbed all the stores in the village. Then they loaded everything onto sleds and left. The commander of the soldiers told the people of the village not to be afraid, that they just wanted to rob from the rich people in the village. He promised not to harm any villagers. The soldiers took everything and were back in Russia before morning. After the soldiers left, the Polish police stayed in the station, because the Russians had told them not to come out of the building. After a long time, the villagers went into the police station to see what had happened to them; only then did they come out of the building.

About seven kilometers from my village was a watchman's building that was also loaded with forest products. It belonged to another Polish noble. One month later, the soldiers went to that place and robbed it also. The Russians told the police not to come out when they left, but the police ran out of the building and began to shoot at the Russians. One Russian soldier was killed in the shooting, but the rest got away with the goods.

A month later, the Russians came back to that same place. My father happened to drive past in his wagon when the Russians were there. They stopped my father and questioned him. After a few minutes they let him go and told him not to look back. The Russians took everything they could find and made the Polish police lie on the floor. The Russian commander told the police that because they had killed one of his men, he was going to shoot two policemen. He shot two of them and told the rest not to follow when he left. This time the Polish police obeyed. After that the Polish government sent in the army, and the Russians stayed out of the area. The Polish Army remained with us until 1926.

Many of the Jews in my village made money by working for the Polish soldiers. They washed their clothes and sold them whatever they needed. The Jews in the village had a clear concept of their Jewish identity. We were Polish citizens, but not Poles. It was the same way with the White Russian farmers. We all got along very well with the Polish Army. There were no problems.

From time to time, Communists would come to our village. They had to be very careful to be sure that the Polish government didn't catch them. If they were caught, they would be taken to Warsaw and put into prison. Life was very difficult for Communists in Polish prisons. They were beaten and many were never heard from again. The Polish government didn't like Communists. After 1939 many of these Communists would be released from jail and put in charge of Polish cities and towns. Some of them were good men but many were not.

My family lived in a small house during these years. It had one large room, and my father partitioned off part of it for my mother and him. We children slept on hard wooden benches and used our coats for blankets. We had two cows and some chickens. We sold our cow manure to the farmers. We ate potatoes and milk most of the time. I enjoyed that food and never became tired of it. Meat was very expensive, and we very rarely ate it.

My grandfather died in 1928. He had a good life and worked hard until the day he died. We all lived together in the same village and the same house. Everyone wanted to be close to his family. That was what was important to us, just the way people felt then.

During this time I worked for my father. I used to travel with a horse and wagon and sell grease from barrels to the farmers who needed it for their wagon wheels. I was not in school because I had turned fifteen. I usually sold two quarts of grease for about forty pounds of potatoes. There was no money involved in the transaction. I just traded my grease to a farmer for whatever he had. It was not an easy job, but I was young, and it was fine for me. I also made some extra money by driving people from the village to the railroad station.

When I was eighteen years old, I had to go register for service with the Polish Army. All the boys took their physicals on the same day: May 15. Most of the farmers' sons were happy to register, but many of the Jews were not so happy. There was no choice, and everyone had to register. When the boys went to the railroad station to go to the army, the whole village went with them to see them off. Everyone was fighting and drinking and having a good time. The women were crying, but the men were usually very proud. I remember a man was playing an accordion and another a banjo and everyone was singing. The villagers still remembered the killing of the colonel but knew they were wrong in that case; and, in any event, they had no choice but to send their sons into the Polish Army. Everyone served willingly in the army, and, until 1939, voiced no open objections. As far as army service was concerned, it was as if the incident with the colonel had never happened.

The inductions took place in the fall. I was not called up in 1931, but had to wait another year before I went into the army. I had saved some money and gave it to my father and told him to send it to me from time to time so I would have some spending money.

 ⊿ ⊾

In 1932, at the age of twenty-one, I began my army service. The only boys who were excused from the army were those with poor eyesight and hearing. Occasionally the army would have enough recruits, and then some lucky boys would escape army service. This was very rare, and not many escaped service in this way. We all accepted army duty, but no one volunteered for it. We had been living in Poland for many years now and could all speak Polish, so there was no language problem.

I found that army life was very strict. There were many rules, and they all had to be obeyed. Soldiers were punished for the most minor infraction of the rules. When I received my draft notice, I had two weeks to report to my regiment along with another boy from my village. The other village boys had to go to another regiment. I had to serve twenty-two months. The army gave me a railroad ticket to get to the camp. On the train we were joined by four hundred other recruits, all going to the same place. Every Polish regiment received new recruits every year, so there were always fresh men coming to serve with the older, more experienced soldiers.

The train went to Warsaw and then to a Polish army base that was located near the German border. There were two non-commissioned officers to meet us when we got off the train. We had to walk through the town and were impressed by what we saw. It was a German town, and the streets and houses were neat and clean. We were all small-town boys or farmers, and it seemed like a big city to us.

We were put in large barracks, each with twenty-four beds. In the middle of the room was a table with two benches. Everyone had a closet for his things. They showed us how to arrange our clothes in the closet down to the last detail. They even had an exact way to hang our swords: there were two nails in the door, and everyone had to hang his sword in exactly the same place. For two days we did nothing, and it was nice. They were polite to us, and we all thought we were on a vacation. The food was good, and the beds were comfortable. We thought we had a good thing with the army.

In the morning we had coffee and bread for breakfast. They gave us our bread the night before, and we could eat it anytime. We usually saved part for the coffee in the morning, but you could eat it all at night if you were hungry. If you had money, you could buy more food from the commissary. One problem we had was that right after we had our breakfast served, we were called out into formation. We hardly had any time to eat. You always had to eat quickly in the army. Lunch was soup with mashed potatoes. Some of the potatoes had pork fat and tasted very good. Supper was soup and coffee. That was what we had to eat. We were always hungry and ate everything the army gave us.

On the second day we were in the army, the major who was in command of the regiment came to see us. We were all scared of him. He walked among us and didn't say a word. We then had to go and get our uniforms and equipment. They gave us our boots, shoes, and clothes without even measuring us. The sergeant would just take a look at us and decide what size we needed, and that was that. You had to take whatever they gave you with no complaints. All the clothes and equipment we had were used. The only time the army ever gave us new equipment or clothes was when we went on leave home or to the town for a few days. After we returned, we always had to turn in the equipment. We had to put our own clothes in boxes and cover everything with moth flakes. The clothes stayed there for two years. We learned to make our own beds, and by the end of the week the vacation was over. We never had a chance to rest after that.

In the morning, we had five minutes to get dressed and make our beds. Everything had to be clean and polished. We were up at six in the morning in the winter. After we were dressed, we went outside and stood in formation for ten minutes while we prayed. We took off our hats and lowered our heads for the prayers. We had to sing the same Polish prayer every morning. Everything had to be correct down to the number of fingers on the rim of the hat.

We then went to the stables to clean the horses. We had two brushes. One was a metal brush, and the other was a bristle brush. We had to clean the whole coat of the horse and comb everything out. That took forty-five minutes, and then we took the horses outside to drink at the pump. The horses ate while we were combing them. At seven, we washed ourselves from the same pump from the waist up. We always had to wash outside no matter what the weather was like. We washed outside even in the winter with the wind and snow. We washed very quickly and then dressed for breakfast.

After breakfast, we had to shine our boots and spurs and clean our rifles. We then lined up for inspection by the major. He checked everything. We next marched to the drill field to practice close-order drills for an hour. By nine we were back in the barracks. From nine to ten, we had outdoor exercise; and from ten to eleven we had lectures concerning Polish history and the Polish Army. At eleven we went back to the horses to clean them again. At eleven-fifty we watered the horses again and went for lunch. From twelve to one, we could do whatever we wanted. Many men went back to the barracks to sleep.

From one to two in the afternoon, we had different things to do every day. For example, one day we might train on our horses and learn to ride while carrying our lances and turning the horse with our feet. From two to three, we still worked with our horses. From three to four, we learned about different types of weapons. We had to know the names of all the weapons and how to operate them. From four to five, we had formation marching on the drill field without our rifles. At five we went back to the stalls to clean the horses again. We cleaned them three times every day. At six we were finished for the day unless there was a special night assignment.

Sometimes we had to work in the regimental office or go into the town on an errand or work with the horses again. I occasionally went on field maneuvers with my regiment. I usually enjoyed being out in the fresh air, except in winter when the snow was deep and it was very cold. Once we were in the field for several weeks with our horses. The best duty to have was in the town guarding some army equipment for twenty-four hours. We were on for six hours and off for six hours. You could sleep or walk around the town when you were free. Sometimes at night I would write letters home or just rest. I would also visit friends who were stationed in different regiments. Everyone had to be back in formation for evening prayers by eight forty-five. By nine we were in bed and fast asleep. I never had any trouble sleeping in the army. I was always tired by the end of the day.

After evening prayers, you could not be outside of the barracks unless you had a special pass. I remember I would wake up by four or five in the morning and go to the bathroom with my wooden shoes. I always ran back to bed as soon as possible. I adjusted easily to army life. Many city boys had a hard time. Some of them cried at night, but they still had to stay. Army life was easier for those of us who came from small villages.

After six weeks, we were officially sworn into the army. There were very few troublemakers in the army. You could go to jail for a few days for a minor infraction of the rules or a few months for talking back to a sergeant. If you hit an officer, they could shoot you. The jail was hard punishment. It consisted of one plain cell with a hard bench. That was all it contained. There was one small window high off the floor, but you couldn't see out of it. If you were in for a long time, you had bread and water to eat and a regular meal only every third day. Every ten days we heard who was in trouble for breaking the rules. We heard who was going to jail and for how long. The whole regiment was lined up in formation to hear the news. We were also paid every ten days.

The army was very strict about their horses. They would put you in jail for a week for not taking care of your horse or mistreating your horse. The horses had English blood and were of the best quality. Many retired army officers raised horses for a living.

In 1933 I went with an officer and three other soldiers to buy horses for the army. We bought seventeen horses. They were strong and young and hard to handle. That was a joy, and the officer took me because I was very good with horses. We left on Saturday and had to return by Tuesday. We had eighteen Zlotys in expense money for every man. We slept in empty army barracks and ate our meals in army kitchens. We could then spend the money and have a good time. That Sunday after I was finished my work, I went to a local zoo. I had never seen such animals before. I bought some cakes to eat and had a good time. It was a beautiful day, and I stayed until the zoo closed at five. Then I walked around the city and returned to the barracks to sleep, but I could have stayed out the entire night if I wanted. At twelve, the officer came in all drunk.

I remember him well. He was forty-three and very strong. He was singing Polish songs the whole night.

Monday morning we picked up the horses and had to leave. I was in charge of two horses and had a hard time with them. There were frightened by all the noise in the city. The officer yelled at some people who were making noises, and they stopped immediately. There was great respect for the army in Poland in those days. I returned to my barracks by three in the morning. I could sleep late that day, and everyone was jealous of me.

Every Saturday morning, the officers took the Jewish boys who didn't have duty into the town to go to the local synagogue. The Christians went to church on Sunday. The Russian Orthodox boys had to go to the Polish Catholic church.

After six months in the army, I was allowed to go home on leave. Not everyone could go home from the army on leave. You had to behave and have a good record. Some men couldn't go because an officer didn't like them. I went home because I was good with the horses, and my officers were proud of me.

Once the major played a trick on a group of new recruits. He called me over to stand in front of them and told them I was the biggest troublemaker in the army. He said I wrote home and complained about the army and told everyone who would listen that they beat me all the time. I was just a lousy guy and a troublemaker, and I couldn't ride at all when I came into the army. After he made this speech, I got on my horse and went through my drills perfectly. I was his example. If he could make a soldier out of me, then anyone could be a good soldier. I almost laughed, but they believed him and it worked.

I went home for Passover and arrived in time for the first Seder. My house looked so small. My father and mother looked at me. I had no stomach, and all of my clothes were from the army. My father looked at my sword and ran his finger along the edge. I had to report to the police station the next day. That was an army rule, and everyone had to report. The police kept their eyes on soldiers who were home on leave. If they caused any trouble, they had to go back to the army right away. Anyone who caused a problem on leave would never be given leave time again by the army. The Jewish boys were usually good when they came home, but sometimes the farmer's sons would get drunk and start to fight and become unruly. The police would come immediately and arrest them and send them right back to the army. I had only one leave the entire time I was in the Polish Army.

By the second year, army life was easier. I had a new major and was in charge of many of the regiment's horses.

But by the end of the second year, everyone was waiting to go home. We counted the weeks and then the days. Sometimes we even counted the number of loaves of bread we would get until we went home. I remember that last morning when I had to turn in my army clothes and put on my civilian clothes. They smelled from moth flakes, and I really looked crazy. I had a free train ticket home, but I started to cry when I left. When I went home on leave, I felt like someone, and now I was a bum dressed in my old clothes going home for good. It was hard to change from being a soldier to a civilian again. It was a strange feeling I had leaving the army. Many of the boys felt the same way. We were counting the days until we got out, and yet we were sad to leave. A few boys stayed in the army for five years and became sergeants and even officers, but most of us just went home. All the Jewish people in the village saw me come home and greeted me. It felt good to be home again, and I soon adjusted to civilian life.

I was twenty-four when I left the army. The house seemed small to me. I looked and looked at the ceiling. It seemed to be just above my head. I was used to the high ceiling of the army barracks. It was many weeks before I became used to that house again. There were no jobs in the village except cutting wood in the forest. It was hard work, and you had to eat pork to do it. For this reason Jews never worked in the forest. What could I do? I had no land and was not a farmer. I finally met a man with a horse, and I would go with him to other villages to buy cattle from the farmers. My father had a kosher butcher store in the village at that time. It was enough for our village. We would sell cattle to my father and the other butcher stores in the town of Luninets. I would also help my father in the store. That was my life. I didn't make much, but I didn't need much.

My father also had two machines that cleaned sheep's wool. The farmers cut the hair off in the fall and brought it to my father's machines to clean. We had wool from all the nearby villages. That was a good business. For six or eight weeks, we worked hard and could make enough to live on for six months. The farmers paid us with food. They gave us potatoes, flour, beans, lentils, chickens, or whatever they had. The farmers stayed in our house until the work was done. We were glad to have them even though they smoked all the time and spit on the floor.

In winter, I would walk from house to house looking for things to buy and sell. I bought horse and squirrel skins. I knew the condition of all the horses in the village and could always tell when one was going to die. I would buy the skin from the farmer and bury the horse in the woods for him. It was hard work to take the skin off, and I had to be careful not to cut or tear the skin, but I was good at it. I could make seven zlotys for one skin— enough to buy two weeks' worth of flour.

I never wanted to leave my village. I was used to life there. I knew all the farmers and was a good friend to many of them. I could go to them and borrow anything I needed. I could borrow hay, food, or tools. We knew each other from childhood and trusted each other. I always paid them back, and they did the same for me. All the farmers kept pigs, and in the winter the pigs lived with them in the houses. All the other animals had to stay in the barn.

In 1937, I had to return to the army for one month to do my reserve duty. I was stationed in Warsaw with another regiment. We never believed there would be a war. In 1938, there was a war scare, but nothing happened. I had a chance to see a lot of Warsaw at that time. Warsaw was a beautiful city, though much of it was destroyed in the Second World War. I heard the Poles rebuilt it after the war. I hope they rebuilt it in the same way it was before the war. I have good memories of Warsaw.

In 1939 we knew something was going to happen. There were no newspapers or radio to tell us what was wrong, but we could sense the uneasiness in the air. We knew nothing about the Germans and heard very little about Hitler before the war. We thought Hitler was the leader of Germany, just like Roosevelt was the leader of the United States.

In the summer of 1939, the Polish government began to call up army reservists for duty at the German frontier. The troops were stationed on the border for the entire summer. My brother was in the army, but I was not called up.

≤ ≥

The war started on September 1, 1939. We had no idea what was happening. We knew the Germans were no good, but we had no idea of what they would do to us. The war was over too quickly. Poland dropped in three weeks, and I was not even called into the army because there wasn't time. For two weeks after the fall of Poland, there was no government in our village. We were near the Russian border and saw no Germans. The police took off their uniforms and hid in the woods. The police were afraid of the Russians and the farmers. The police would beat the farmers from time to time, and now that there was no government they were afraid the farmers would take their revenge on them. They hid in the woods to see what was happening.

The Jews in the village were very scared and did not know what was going to happen to them. Some people hated the Jews, and with no government anything could happen. The village formed a local government for a time. The people were good because they remembered the incident with the colonel and did not want any trouble.

Two weeks later a Russian truck came to my village. The Russians were fixing the phone lines. We knew that everything would be taken care of now. We ran to the truck and began to talk to the soldiers. One of them was Jewish, and we asked him many questions. We asked him what life was like in Russia for the Jews. We had not heard anything about Russia for over twenty years. He told us not to worry. Everyone would have a job; everyone worked for the government. It sounded good to us.

I was also married during this time. I had married a local girl whom I had known all my life, and we moved into a small home. I had wanted to get married for a long time, but I took a long time to get up the courage to ask. I had twin sons who were born in 1940, and I was very proud of them.[5]

---

5   Editor's Note: Dr. Butowsky notes, "This was all I could get Mr. Neiman to say about his first wife and children. The subject was just too difficult for him to talk about."

Mr. Neiman's wife's name was Lea Neiman (née Osherovski), and his twin sons' names were Avraham (or Aharon) and Yaakov. In the course of research for this project, we located Pages of Testimony that Mr. Neiman filled out in 1969 for Yad Vashem's Central Database of Shoah Victims' Names. These documents record the names and some personal information about ten members of Mr. Neiman's family who were murdered during the Holocaust and one who was murdered in the United States at an earlier time. More information about Mr. Neiman's family and this archive may be found in the Appendix below.

Chapter Four

The Russian Occupation

Before the Russians came to our village in 1939, all the Jews were walking around like lambs. We were all afraid of what was going to happen to us. Even the farmers were scared. They remembered the colonel and were afraid to do anything.

One day we saw two Russian soldiers, and they told us not to worry. We felt better after that. The Russians sent a Jewish Communist named Joseph Flaxman to organize our village for the government. He began to make many rules and regulations for the whole village, and we felt more secure. Flaxman was from the city of Lublin and had been a Communist before the war. The Poles caught him, and he spent five years in a Polish jail for Communist activities. It was a terrible jail, and he suffered during those years. The Poles did terrible things to Communists in that jail, and many who went in were never heard from again. We heard that they beat people and kept them in small cells for long periods of time.

We still had our Polish money, and the Russians told the store owners to sell what they had to the people and to take the Polish money in payment. The storekeepers didn't like the idea, but they had to obey the government. Many of them wanted to hide their merchandise or sell it for Russian rubles. A few managed to keep part of their stock, but most were forced to sell out. They hoped they would be able to exchange their Polish money later for Russian money. They began to sell out and hid whatever they could. They were afraid to leave the shelves empty. Soon there was nothing left to sell, and the storekeepers couldn't buy any more goods, so they closed.

Three months after the start of the Russian occupation, the government told us to throw our Polish money away. It was no longer good for anything. My father and I didn't have any money, so we didn't worry. Some people had American money, and they were lucky. American money was good all the time; it was the only money we trusted.

The Russians opened the border, and we could now visit relatives and friends we hadn't seen in twenty years. The borders were not open as they are here between the United States and Canada. You had to go to the government and fill out many forms before they would give you a piece of paper to cross for a short visit. We asked everyone who came over what was happening in Russia. The government told us everything was good in Russia, and all the people were happy under Communism. We heard a different story from the Russian people. They told us that you could not talk in Russia or say anything of a political nature. They said that many people went to jail and were never seen again. The Russian police usually arrested people late at night or early in the morning. They knocked on your door and gave you ten minutes to pack up and leave. Very often they took entire families and left the home deserted. Most of the people who were arrested didn't even know why they were arrested. Those who had been in Russia told us that the government took everything they had before the Revolution. You could have one cow and a small garden, and that was all. Everyone had to work on the collective farm and keep his mouth shut. If you were educated you might get a government job, but the middle class was in bad shape.

The Russians treated us differently at first, and we hoped that things would not be difficult. This soon changed. The government went first to the storekeepers and anyone who had money and made them give contributions to the government. They would send a note to you to come to the government office the next day and pay five thousand rubles. Many families in the village were picked up at night and taken away. Everyone was scared. The government also picked up all the Polish government workers and intellectuals. Some people ran away but most were caught by the Russians. They all were sent into Deep Russia to work on a collective farm. Even the smallest tailors and shoemakers who worked alone were arrested as exploiters of the people. Everything was mixed up.

That winter they sent the farmers into the woods to work for the government. They had to chop wood for the government. Everything was for the government. The Russians put everything we produced on trains and sent it to Russia. Everyone in the village had his wood quota. If you were sick or had no horse you had to hire some-one to fill your wood quota. Many horses died that first winter. They had to work hard all winter, and we did not have enough food to feed them.

All of the Polish policemen ran away or were arrested by the Russians. The Russians hired many local boys, including some Jews, to be policemen. They could be nice to you or get you in trouble. If they reported you, the Russians would come to your house at two in the morning and tell you to get dressed. You were under arrest and put onto a train that went deep into Russia, usually Siberia. Later the Russians would come and arrest the remaining members of your family, who would also be sent to Siberia. Those who were arrested did not know it, but the Russians saved their lives. They were deep in Russia when the Germans attacked, and so they were safe. They survived the war.

The Russians also looked for people who had two houses and usually took one house. If they thought you were rich or had many possessions, they would send you a bill for 10,000 rubles. You had to pay; there was no choice.

If they thought you had more money, then you would get another bill. Everyone was trying to hide their money and goods. Many people ran away to the forest to escape.

⚜ ⚜

During that first winter, the border between the Russians and the Germans was watched very carefully. It was difficult to cross. Still, many Jews on the German side of the border began to flee to the Russian side. They were usually young and came alone. It was impossible to flee with your family. There were too many people for the crossing, and someone was always old or sick. The Germans were killing Jews even at that time. They killed Jews at any time during the day or night, and they made the Jews do hard physical work for free. Every morning there were dead Jews in the streets of German-occupied Poland. It was a terrible time, but not as bad as it would become two years later. The Germans were not rounding up the Jews yet.

Every Jewish family took in two or three Jews. They had no money or clothes, so we had to support them. We took in a few of the youngsters. There were about ten of these children in our village. Some of them became homesick and received letters telling them to come home. A few went home and were later killed by the Germans.

Later that winter of 1939-40 the Russians put up posters telling the Jews who had fled the Germans that they could go back home. They had a train and passes for all who wanted to return. Some tried to cross the border alone and were caught and sent deep into Russia. The ones who were caught were lucky.

In 1940, the Russians put up posters again telling the runaways that if they wanted to go home, the Russians would help them. They would be put on special trains and sent home. Many people signed up for the trains. One month later the Russians used the lists to arrest everyone at night and send them into Deep Russia. They never got home again. Some were sent to the Persian border and were lucky. It was warm there. The unlucky ones were sent to Siberia. The Russians really saved their lives. When the Germans came in 1941, they were safe in Russia.

Those who went home were all killed.

The Russians were not against the Jews like the Germans were. Everyone suffered under the Russians. When the Russians started their collective farms, there was great suffering among the peasants. It was terrible. We heard about it from the farmers who survived. The Russians were equally hard on everyone.

⚒ ⚒

During this time, I was working as a butcher. I traveled with my horse and wagon to the farmers to buy cattle, which I brought back to the village to slaughter. I ran a kosher shop. The Russians didn't stop me. They told me I could continue with my business. Many other butchers were frightened and stopped working, but I continued with my work. I was small, and I hoped they would forget about me. I had a friend from my army days who had a brother who was a Communist in the government, and my friend promised to ask his brother to tell him when I should stop working. My brother's friend had a good job with the government. He traveled from village to village and collected tax money from the people. That was an easy job. Everyone paid on time with no complaints. Anyone who objected would be picked up a few days later and sent into Russia. Very few people ever objected. I slaughtered my cattle and did a good business. The farmers were all anxious to sell cattle. The job was a little dangerous, but I was willing to take a chance. In 1941 my friend told me it was time to stop, and I went out of business. I began to help my father as a carpenter. I worked on the windows and floors of new homes my father was building. My father needed my help and paid me thirty rubles a day.

Next to our house lived a shoemaker from Brest-Litovsk. His name was Abbi. He had a nice boy about nine years old. Abbi told me he had a sister in Brest-Litovsk and said we could take food to the city to sell and make ourselves some money. It was impossible for people in the city to buy what they needed from the government, so it would be easy for us to sell our food.

I decided to go with him and took butter, soap, kielbasa, and cows' hooves to make yogurt. I took two suitcases and a bag with food that I carried on my back. I had about ninety pounds of food with me. We also took some women's rubbers that we found in the village. He told me that people in the city would buy anything we had, even if they didn't need it right now. You might need something in the future and not be able to buy it. There were only government stores, and they always were short of goods. Many times, people in the cities would wait in lines for hours only to find that a store was sold out.

We hired a farmer with a horse and sled to take us to Luninets where the train stopped. It was winter and was very cold. I realized that what I was doing was dangerous, but I wanted to try it. Selling in the city was strictly illegal. The train arrived at midnight. When it stopped, my partner got on with no trouble, but a woman conductor saw me get on with my packages, and she began to shout at me. She called me a speculator. I didn't know what to do. I could have just left everything on the train and run away, but I decided to stay. She was not a policeman, and it was none of her business what I had in my packages. She kept calling me a speculator. I told her I was going to visit my sister and gave her two pieces of kielbasa. She went away, and I stayed on the train. I was on my way to Brest-Litovsk to trade.

We got into Brest-Litovsk at midnight and were in a huge train station that was built during the time of the

Tsars. It was very quiet in the station, and only twelve people got off the train. We had to walk through the station to the other side of the city. There was no public transportation at that time of night except for some men driving old wagons in front of the station. We decided to walk. My partner told me that his sister's house was close. It was very cold and snowing, and I was breathing hard from all the weight I had to carry. We walked through the empty streets and were about one block from the station when I saw a young man coming over to us. He wore a uniform and carried a shotgun. He was a Jewish policeman. He stopped a man walking in front of us and asked to see his papers. He stopped us and asked to see our papers too. After a few minutes, he told the three of us that we had to follow him to the police station. I felt like dropping everything I had and running away, but I was unfamiliar with the city and would soon get lost. My friend told him we were just visiting his sister, but the policeman made us follow him anyway. I was carrying eighty pounds of food, and there was snow on the ground.

We walked almost two miles before we came to a large house that served as the police station. The policeman took us inside and told us to stand by the door and wait for him. He took the other fellow in a back room and began to question him. I was scared and didn't know what to do. I had to think fast before I was in trouble. My heart was beating very hard, and I decided to walk down the corridor to see what was happening in the back rooms. I saw a lot of packages in the hallway just like the ones I had. The police were checking them. I knew I was in serious trouble. I had many packages full of food, and I did not want to be charged as a speculator. I went back to my friend, who still was standing by the door, and told him what I saw. He didn't know what to say or do. He just stood there scared to do anything at all. I told him I wanted to run. He said I was crazy and should stay put. I picked up my bags and walked out the front door and away from the police station as fast as my legs would carry me.

My friend stayed. I didn't know where to go. I just wanted to get away. After I was away from the police, I could worry about my future. I walked across the street and was immediately stopped by two men who wanted to buy my packages. I told them no and continued to walk. I thought they might be more policemen, and I only wanted to get away as fast as possible. I started walking in the direction of the train station. I was stupid, I thought to myself. I should have left the packages in the station, but I did not want to lose them. They would only attract attention to me in the street. I walked another block when I heard someone following me. I turned and saw my friend. He said that when he saw no one come after me, he also left. We went to his sister's house and got there by four in the morning. She took everything from us and sold it within a few hours. I didn't make much money on that trip. When I got home I made up my mind not to do it again. I had had enough of the Russians and their rules against speculation.

The winter passed, and in the spring of 1941 the Russians asked me to go to the farmers and buy cattle for the government. They gave me thirty thousand rubles and an official stamp book. I didn't want the job, but I had no choice. I hired a horse and wagon and went from village to village to buy cattle. I knew all the farmers and within a few days had bought thirty-one head of cattle. I had to hire a couple of men to help me. I paid for the cattle by weight, and during the trip home they lost weight. When they weighed the cattle the next day, they were short weight. They also changed the grade that I paid for and told me that I had cheated the government by three thousand rubles. There was no way I could win. Either I cheated the government, or the government would say I cheated the farmers. Either way, I was in trouble.

It seemed like everyone was in trouble with the Russians. You had to be very careful, and you could still get in trouble.

That happened in May 1941, and they told me I would have a trial for cheating the government. The war started the next month, and I never did have my trial.

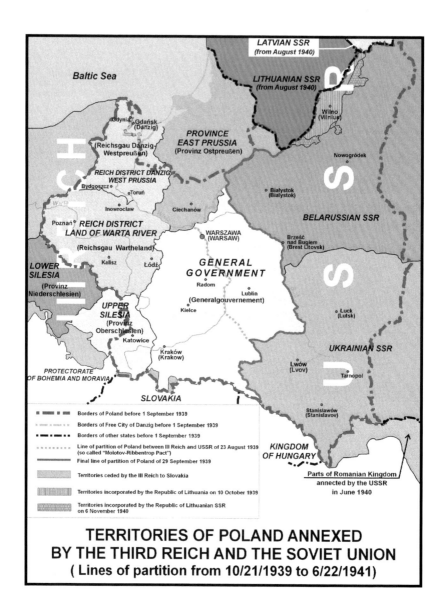

TERRITORIES OF POLAND ANNEXED
BY THE THIRD REICH AND THE SOVIET UNION
(Lines of partition from 10/21/1939 to 6/22/1941)

Chapter Five

I Join the Russian Army

The war started on the night of June 21, 1941. Even before the war, we suspected that something was going to happen. The Russians kept telling us not to worry; they were strong and would beat the Germans. We never believed that something would happen to us. We just didn't know that much about what was happening in the world. We had very little information except what the Russians told us. They told us that they were strong. The people in the towns knew more than us. We found out what information we could by word of mouth from government officials who had access to more information. All we knew was that there were problems between the Russians and the Germans. We didn't know what the problems were, but we could sense the tension.

For months before the start of the war, I could see tanks and men riding the trains and traveling the roads from Pinsk to the frontier. They traveled only at night and were careful not to be seen during the day. But I saw them anyway. You couldn't hide that much equipment and that many men. We knew that Germany was already at war with France and England and could see the Russian Army preparing for war during the winter of 1940-1941. The war material seemed endless, and it all went to the German border. The Russians told us nothing about the Germans, but we heard stories from Jews who fled from the German-occupied part of Poland. The Germans were killing Jews and leaving their bodies in the streets. The only thing the Russians told us was that they were strong and would beat the heads of the Germans. We believed them. After all, they had so many tanks and men on the border.

I remember the night the war started. It was warm and everyone was walking outside in the streets of the village. There was a little rain in the air. The police told us to put out our lights. We could hear airplanes flying overhead in the direction of Brest-Litovsk. We knew on the night of June 21, 1941, that Russia and Germany were at war. The Jews were worried and walked around outside under a large tree. The Russian farmers were happy and prayed that the Germans would come quickly. They hated the Communists and wanted to be free of them. We Jews knew better and feared for our lives. We didn't know what we should do. The Germans had done unbelievable things to the Jews in their part of Poland, and we heard about them. We were right on the front line and had no place to run.

Six days later, the Germans were in our village. There was no person to tell us what we should do. The police ran away. They had connections and were warned about the true military situation and ran for their lives. All night long, the planes were flying and bombing. They created a good deal of panic among the civilian population.

The only way to run was to take some food from the house and put it in a large sack and start walking. We had no horses, and there were woods all around the village. My father was fifty-seven, and my mother was fifty-four. They were middle-aged people and couldn't run. Many younger people had small children and couldn't run. The only people who had a chance were youngsters who were free to run away and had only themselves to care for. The rest had to stay and wait for the Germans. We didn't know what we should do. Who could ever believe that the Germans would kill everyone just because they were Jewish? Just killing Jews for no reason—that did not make any sense.

We walked around under that tree until one in the morning. Then we went to bed. We thought that in the morning we would have more information and know better what we should do. At two in the morning I heard a knock on my window. I wasn't sleeping. It was a Russian boy who was a neighbor of mine. He was a member of our village government. He told me that I was drafted into the army and had to report to the train station by eleven in the morning.

It was now official: war with Germany. I was awake and couldn't sleep. At three, my father came to my house and talked to me. There was nothing we could do, and I knew I had to go into the army. We all felt so helpless. My brother was drafted into the army also, but he was not home at the time. He was in the town of Luninets and came home later the next day and went right into the army. The Russians were picking up all the men they could before they left. Everything was a mess. No one knew what was happening or what to do. Everything was mixed up. Everything was in confusion.

The control of the Russian government over our village began to dissolve almost immediately. Many farmers refused to go into the army. They wanted the Germans to come. They didn't know about the Germans, but they hated the Communists. The Jews were worried about the lack of government because without it anything could happen. The Russian farmers could come and rob and kill us. The farmers believed that all the Jews had money and were rich. Our village remained quiet. The farmers remembered the colonel and were careful to be good. The Poles taught them a good lesson.

⨉ ⨉

The Russian farmers had deep feelings against the Jews. Your local boys could be trusted, but Russians from other villages could come to kill and rob. I remember an example of this hatred that happened to me before the war. When the Russians came to our village in 1939, they closed the church and forced the priest to move away. The priest was a man about forty and was a well-liked person in the village. I knew him well. He had a house and some land that the village gave him. He had no choice and had to leave. I went to see him when I heard that he was going and offered to buy his stock of winter potatoes. He had prepared them before he knew he had to go. I bought the potatoes and began to dig them out of the ground. It cost me four hundred rubles for two large piles of potatoes. I was standing near the potatoes when a Russian neighbor of mine came up to talk to me. He was a good man, and I knew him well. His name was Siter, and he was a quiet fellow. He wanted to buy the potatoes, but he came too late. He was very angry and looked at me and said that what I needed was Hitler. He kept saying that all the Jews in the village needed Hitler. I could have reported him to the government and gotten him in trouble, but he was a friend of mine, and I decided not to do it. I never forgot the incident. The Russian farmers could change from being your friend to being an enemy overnight. You never knew what they would do.

Americans don't really understand the war. Here you go to war and read about it in the newspapers. You eat well and sleep well, and no one bombs you. Over there it was different. Everything was mixed up. People were taken from their homes and never seen again. The Jews were scared. Only the Russian farmers didn't seem to worry. They had their land and houses and were determined to stay. The Germans wouldn't hurt them. Many of the Jewish houses were occupied later by German soldiers and were blown up by the partisans [members of the resistance] during the war. There were many partisans in the woods. Many Jews were with them.

I know one man who was with the partisans. He was from Gonshan, a village near us. Late in the fall of 1941, he found a little Jewish boy, who was about thirteen years old and was from our village, in the woods. His name was Chici, and his father was a good friend of mine. His father and mother and sister were all killed by the Germans, but Chici managed to get away. My friend knew Chici's father and took care of him in the woods. It was cold that winter, and Chici had no warm clothes or shoes. Chici and two other men would sneak into the village to spy on the Germans. Once they found a group of German soldiers in a farmhouse and told the farmer to leave. Then they blew up the house with the Germans inside. The partisans gave Chici a big shotgun to carry that would touch the ground when he walked. It began to snow, and there were many days when the temperature was very cold. Chici could not keep warm or dry. The partisans were under heavy pressure from the Germans and had to keep moving all the time. There was no chance to rest or sleep. Chici contracted typhus and became very ill. My friend found a farmer's haystack and told Chici to hide in it. He had a high temperature and could not move. The Germans put constant pressure on the partisans, and they had to move. Chici hid in the middle of the haystack with little food. Chici died alone in that haystack. The farmer found him in the spring. I knew this little boy. I went to his bris[6] when he was born, and his family was good friends with mine. He didn't do anything to the Germans, and he had to die alone.[7]

That morning the whole village went to the train with the men who were drafted into the army. Many men never came, but there was still a large crowd of people. I couldn't even take my good boots. They were in the repair shop in Luninets, and there was no way to get them. The whole village seemed to be crying, but there was nothing that we could do. My grandmother walked

---

6   Editor's Note: A bris is the "covenant of circumcision": a Jewish religious male circumcision ceremony performed by a mohel on the eighth day of a male infant's life.
7   Editor's Note: Mr. Neiman had a difficult time telling me this story. He was very emotional, and we had to stop several times.

with me and my wife, and my mother and sister walked in front carrying my two young sons. My grandmother took a twig from a bush and told me to hold it up when they called my name. It was supposed to bring me good luck. I did it for her. Perhaps she was right. I kissed by family goodbye and got on the train. Soon they were all dead. The Germans killed the men soon after they came to the village, and the women and children were taken to the town of Luninets and put into a ghetto. They were killed in 1942. I was in the army and heard about it later.

I never saw my village again. It was destroyed by the Germans. The village was rebuilt after the war, but I never went back. It was too dangerous to do so. Even after the war, many Jews were killed when they tried to return to their homes in Poland and in Russia. The people just didn't want us to come back. They took everything we had and didn't want to have to answer any questions. It was best not to return. I never saw my family or home again. It was all gone, destroyed by the Germans and the war.

The train took us to Luninets. To this day, I can still hear that train. I can hear the sound of the wheels against the metal tracks. When we arrived in Luninets we found the village deserted. I ran to my uncle's house, which was located near the station. I had some time to wait for the next train. The house was empty. I looked around and heard someone calling my name, "Yitzkhak, Yitzkhak, Yitzkhak!" It was my aunt calling me from another house. She was staying at a neighbor's house with her daughter during the day. Her house had a large shining roof, and she was afraid the Germans would drop a bomb on it. She told me that her daughter and grandson had come that morning and had gone with my uncle to Vautin, which was located in the woods, to be safe from the Germans. My uncle's son ran away that morning to follow the retreating Russians. I returned to the train. The neighbor told me she was worried about her husband, who was a conductor with the railroad. He had been gone for several days, and she was worried that he was hurt and unable to return.

At five that evening we were told that we would have to walk. The Germans had bombed all the trains. We waited until nine when it was good and dark and began to walk along the train tracks. They told us to run into the woods if we heard any German planes. While we were walking, we passed many people traveling the other way. They had been caught away from home by the start of the war and were trying to get home. I am almost sure I saw my aunt from my village pass me in the dark. She was walking with a man who was helping her. It was only an instant, and she was gone. I never saw her again. I don't know what happened to her.

My aunt hid with a neighbor in a Polish home. The Germans found her in 1942 and sent her to Auschwitz where she died. I do not know what happened to the Polish family that hid her for several months. The Germans usually killed any Poles they found hiding Jews, but many Poles did so anyway.

We had a Russian woman lieutenant in charge of us with two local boys helping her. By five the next morning we started walking again. We went to the police station and were told to wait behind the high school. We sat down on the grass and waited for three days. We had nothing to eat, and we slept out in the open. The only thing the Russians gave us was a blanket. After three days, they let us sleep in some empty homes. On June 26, 1941, we left Luninets. We were still walking. There were no trains running. The Germans had destroyed them all.

We could sense that the Germans were close. We walked fourteen kilometers the next day and another six the following day. We were tired of walking and stopped in some empty Jewish homes to rest. All the Jews were crying. No one knew what to do. The Russian government had just disappeared.

I saw my old teacher during this time. He had two children and told them to run away and save their lives. Many Jews ran to the Jewish cemetery and were crying on the graves of their parents. They were asking their parents to save them. The roads were clogged with people by this time. Everyone wanted to get away from the

Germans. Only the old people were staying. Everyone else was running away.

The Russians told us to stay in empty houses. The houses were a mess. It was already six days into the war, and people were already using the houses for latrines. We had to stay in them anyway. We put grass on the floor. Some of the Russian boys were beginning to run away. There was one Russian boy who was a wiseguy.[8] He was working with the Russian government even before the war. He kept telling the lieutenant that he had to watch us carefully to see that we didn't run away. He helped watch us. When we got up that morning he was gone. He ran away during the night. Many Russian boys stayed because they were not sure how the war was going. They thought the Russian Army would begin to push back the Germans, and they would be in trouble for running away. After the sixth day of the war, they were sure the Germans were going to win and began to run away.

There was traffic on the roads all day and night. Some of the more fortunate people had wagons with cows. The next day we were in a small village near the border. The Russians put us on a train. We could see bomb damage everywhere. I saw my uncle's neighbor at that time. He was a train conductor and had a bandage on his head. He was hurt. I didn't have a chance to talk to him and tell him I had talked to his wife a few days before.

---

8   Editor's Note: Mr. Neiman refers to troublemakers and criminals as "wiseguys."

During the trip I saw the mohel who had circumcised my twin sons only nine months before. He was walking on the road fleeing the Germans. I felt very bad when I saw him. I thought I would drop dead. I began to think about my family. He was walking with two other religious Jews and had stopped to draw some water from a well. I couldn't talk to him either.

The Russians were not letting people cross the border. Later, when the Germans came close, the guards fled and anyone could cross into Russia.

When we arrived in the city of Grodno we found it deserted. We were there for ten days and spent most of that time trying to find some food. There was nothing to eat. It was hard to find even a piece of bread.

Chapter Six

The War

The Russians kept marching us deeper and deeper into Russia. Everywhere I went I saw the same story: Russian villages destroyed by German planes, and Russian Jews fleeing from the German Army. Men, women and children were all running from the Germans. The lucky ones had horses and wagons; the rest had to flee on foot. Every few kilometers, the Germans would bomb us. We were now on a train and had to be very careful of the planes. We went to the city of Gomel, which was about one hundred seventy kilometers from my home. The city had been bombed by the Germans the week before and was in ruins. I was there for three days. I then went to the city of Nezhin and was there for about three weeks. The Russians made us take apart a margarine factory for shipment into Deep Russia. We slept in trenches in the woods. We still did not have any Russian army uniforms. Later we were given uniforms. They told us to put our civilian clothes and personal belongings in a bag with our name, and they would send it home. We knew it was a lie. Our homes were already destroyed and overrun by the Germans. I traded my good leather boots for a loaf of bread and some milk.

It was now July 1941, and it was very warm in the woods. We had to be quiet at night, because the Germans were dropping spies into the woods. These men would try to find us and call in the German planes to bomb us. We were only a short distance from the front and could hear the firing all through the night. We saw many Russian soldiers heading for the front. The trucks seemed endless. We could hear the Germans calling from the woods, "Kamerad, Kamerad, komm her!"

I saw a Russian officer yelling at a man in our group who was crying. The man was afraid for his family. The officer told him to forget his family and just think about his duty. He told him that the trench he was digging was now his family. It was his wife, mother, father, children, and he had to forget about everything else. The officer told him everything he had was gone and to forget about it.

We kept moving away from the front. The Russians now gave us guns and ammunition. We were in Poltava, which was a large Russian army base before the war. The Russians were moving all their supplies and equipment into the woods to be safe from the German planes. The base was a tremendous place. Our group of men from Poland now numbered about eighty, and we worked day and night moving supplies into the woods. We also had to load trucks with supplies for the front. We were working hard and were tired. Some of the shells were so large that two men were necessary to lift them. We for worked four hours and rested for four hours. We never stopped working.

There were large tanks of gasoline in the woods with pipes that went through the woods to places where trucks could refuel. The German planes were over us all the time trying to find the supplies. We knew that they were looking for us, but we felt safer in the woods. We had to guard the pipes in addition to our work details. The Russians told us that if we heard knocking on the pipes, we were not to shoot. The Russian officers would patrol the pipes at night and knock on them to signal the guards of their approach. Only if we saw someone near the pipes with no recognition knock could we shoot. I was on guard duty by the pipes one night when I saw a man walking through the woods. He didn't knock on the pipes. I called out to him and told him to stop, but he kept moving. I couldn't see very well in the dark, but I knew someone was there. I heard a lot of noise and then saw him run. I shot twice at him, but missed. He kept running. Eventually it was quiet again. Ten minutes later I heard knocking on the pipes, and a Russian officer approached me to see why I was shooting. I told him what I saw, and he went away. The next day I was called into headquarters and told I was to be given five days in jail for firing my rifle. I was happy. I had a good rest there. I slept on the floor and had good bread to eat. They should have given me ten days in jail. That was my first real rest since the start of the war. Everyone wanted to be in jail. After three days, I was released and went back to work in the woods.

The Germans were coming closer again, and we had to move. Many civilians were moving with us. One day my group was crossing a bridge that was loaded with troops and civilians when a German plane came over and dropped a bomb in the middle of the bridge. I was lucky and got off safely. The bridge began to twist, and the metal turned hot. People, horses, and wagons all went into the water. Everyone was screaming. I never saw so many people killed before. It was a terrible sight. Many people were just blown to pieces.

The army put us on another train and took us back to the city of Gomel. All the soldiers were eating and drinking. Many of them were drunk. The train stopped suddenly, and a Russian lieutenant fell between the cars, cut in half by the wheels. The train stopped to pull him off the tracks. That was the first time I saw a man die close up. He was just laying there on the ground, cut in two. His eyes kept opening and closing. They took his belt, gun, shoes, and papers and just left him there. He was dead, and there was no time to bury him. He had a nice picture of his family that was taken before the war. He was so young, and now he was dead. His eyes kept moving for five minutes.

The train stopped at a little train station, and we were ordered off the train to dig trenches. The Germans bombed us so much there that we became very used to the planes. If no planes came to bomb us, we would wonder where they were. My brother was with me at that time, and he fell down while working and hurt his arm. There was no doctor to help him. He had a difficult time walking. I tied his arm up the best way I could and hoped it would heal. I carried his rifle and equipment.

We were moved again to another town called Sumy. We arrived there early in the morning and had to wait at the train station. There were seven trains in the station, and they were waiting for the tracks to clear. Each train had about sixty or seventy cars carrying troops and supplies. They were all going in different directions. It was a busy station. One train was a hospital train full of wounded soldiers. Suddenly we heard planes overhead, German planes. The Russian officers told us to stay on the trains and be quiet. There were two German planes, and they looked at us for a few minutes and went away. Five minutes later, many German planes came back and began to bomb the station. Everyone jumped off the trains and began to run as fast as possible towards the woods. Bombs were falling all around me, and I thought I was going to be killed. I saw many people killed that day. Women and children were blown to pieces by the bombs. There was food and ammunition lying all over the station, and you could take whatever you wanted. My friend Bronisław, who was with me in the Polish Army, was killed there. His brother was the Communist Flaxman who warned me to stop working as a butcher before the war. My cousin was killed there. My brother and I were separated after that bombing. We ran in opposite directions. I heard later that the stationmaster gave the Germans the signal to bomb the station. He was a Communist and a Party member. They found him out right away and shot him. I don't know how they found him out, but they did.

I began to search for my brother as soon as the bombing stopped. We were lucky and found each other again. Many people became separated in the war and never found each other again. Many women lost their children and could never find them. Some were killed, and some were lost.

Slowly we Jews began to get together again. We crossed to the other side of the woods and found more people. We didn't know what to do now, and there was no one to tell us. The whole group was destroyed. There were just small groups of men wandering around the station. We wanted to stay away from the Germans. The German planes came back again and dropped more bombs, but no one was killed this time. We made our way to a small Russian village about four kilometers from the station. There were about eight of us walking together. Some were Russian boys from my village. We hoped we would be safe there. The Russians in the village were waiting for the Germans. They put white sheets on the roof to signal the Germans not to bomb. They wanted the Germans to come. They didn't know that the Germans would give them a hard time.

There was plenty of food in the village. The corn was high, and all the houses had gardens. The Russian boys wanted to get away from us and go home. They didn't want to be caught by the Germans with a group of Jews. They knew it was dangerous to be with Jews. They could live with the Germans and just wanted to go home. They left us. They told us to wait on one side of the road while they crossed to check it out. They said they would signal us. It was all a lie. When they had the chance, they ran away. We said, "The hell with them!" We didn't care about them. We couldn't go home anyway; we were stuck in Russia.

We decided to go into the Russian village to get some food. It was about six at night. We slept in the cornfields until morning. The next morning we washed ourselves and went into the village to find food. The women of the village gave us cooked blueberries and potatoes. One of our boys looked very Jewish, and the women told him they had no more food. We shared our food with him. We told the women we were from Poland and were lost from our units. They didn't know we were all Jewish.

We walked down a dirt road away from the village and sat on the grass wondering what to do when we saw something from God. We saw a group of soldiers coming toward us and recognized more Jewish friends from the city of Luninets. We were happy to find each other and cried.

We walked to another small town. We were tired and sat under a large tree to rest. My brother was still hurt, and I was worried about him. I found an old woman in the town and paid her ten rubles to pray for him. She prayed for sick people in the town, and I hoped she could help my brother. We saw groups of Russian soldiers everywhere. They were all lost and had no direction. A few days later, while we were still there, some Russian officers found us and we were back in the army again. They were going around the town collecting all the loose soldiers they could find. They put us in a deserted church. Horses had been stabled in the church before us, and the place was filthy. The walls had niches for caskets and urns, so we slept in the walls. We kept moving away from the Germans. Everyone was happy to stay away from the front line. We all wanted to survive the war, and we knew that if we went into the front line, we were dead. The loss of life was unbelievable.

We came to a small village. Many of the houses were empty, so we stayed in them. There were many fruit trees in that town, and we had enough to eat. Then we went to another village and saw a large building and was told it was a mental institution. The inmates were walking around and doing crazy things. There was no one to look after them; the attendants had all run away from the Germans.

We kept walking away from the Germans. That was the main thing. The Russian officers were not anxious to go to the front either, so they kept pushing us to the rear. We were their excuse to stay alive and away from the fighting. Without us they would be dead. Everyone wanted to stay out of the front line, but you had to have a good reason to avoid the fighting. It was impossible to just run away. Many men tried to run but were caught by the Russians and shot. As long as the officers could say they were taking us to the rear to reorganize, we were all safe. All that summer of 1941, we walked away from the Germans to the rear to reorganize, but the Germans never gave us a chance to reorganize. They were always close behind us.

We worked in the woods many times loading supplies for the army. It was hard work, but at least we were safe from the war. We never saw any Germans, but at night we heard them calling, "Kamerad, komm her! Kamerad, komm her!" We never saw them. We saw many trains full of wounded soldiers returning from the front. We found a cow in the woods just as the temperature began to drop. We killed it and cooked the meat. It was good, and we had our first decent meal in many weeks.

Chapter Seven

I Join the Polish Army Again

We were close to the front line and could hear the shooting all the time. The noise never stopped. There were Russian soldiers all around us. Most were heading toward the front, but many were walking away. Some were wounded, but many looked fine. I guess they just did not want to fight anymore. Everyone was scared.

We now went to the city of Tula, which was located about one hundred and fifty kilometers from Moscow. The Russians in charge of us didn't know what they were doing most of the time and were not sure what to do with us because we were Polish citizens. The Russians were not easy to be with, but they were a lot better than the Germans. We just kept walking away from the front line. No one wanted to be near the fighting. The Russian lieutenants in charge of us were happy to have us because we were their excuse for staying out of the war. We were sixty men, all from Poland. Many of us were Jews.

We saw many large armies near Moscow. We walked all around them. No one told us to join any of the armies, so we just kept marching away from the front line. The Russians put us on a train and sent us to another town even further from the front. Moscow was a very dangerous place to be at this time, because the Germans were approaching the city. There was fighting in this area. The time was now November 1, 1941, and the temperature was cold. For the first time, I felt safe from the Germans.

The Russians took me and eleven other men from the group into the woods to load ammunition onto cargo trains. We had a lieutenant and one sergeant over us. The ammunition was heavy and the work hard, but I was alive. I was working near the Don River. I saw fresh Russian armies all over the area. They were preparing to move out and fight the Germans. I felt safe, because I knew they were between me and the Germans. The Russians were preparing to use the ammunition on the Germans in the Battle for Moscow in December 1941.

A larger group of Poles joined my group, and I continued my work. The weather was now bitter cold, and I began to suffer from the exposure. I was living in a train at night and worked loading ammunition during the day. The front line was moving again in my direction, and I began to worry. By December, the front was less than thirty kilometers from me. I was afraid that the Russians would put me into the front line. Many Polish citizens had to go to the front to fight. Others were sent deep into Russia to work. There was no way to know what the Russians would do with me.

＊ ＊

I was living near a small village at that time, and the women of the village let me cook food in their kitchens. I never had enough to eat and was hungry all the time. At night I would try to steal some food from the trains. The lieutenant and the sergeant spent most of their time in the village with the women drinking. They had a good time.

Once I stole a bag of flour. It weighed one hundred sixty pounds. I took it into the village and traded it for what I needed. Later I found an unguarded train full of good Russian vodka and helped myself. I gave some of it to the lieutenant and the sergeant and used the rest for myself to keep warm at night. There were never enough men to guard the trains at night, and there was a lot of stealing from the government. After all, they paid us nothing for our work, so we felt justified in taking what we needed to survive. The guards could always be bribed and would turn their heads the other way for the right price. Many times we were the guards and could steal what we needed at our leisure.

The lieutenant gave me an army requisition for a cow. I went to the local collective and took a cow. They had to give it to me with no questions asked. The army could take whatever it wanted from the collectives. I slaughtered it outside in the cold and cut up the meat. It was difficult work, and I had to drink a lot of vodka to keep warm while I worked.

One day my brother was ordered to take some supplies to the front line. I went to the lieutenant and asked him to find someone else for the job. I was afraid that something would happen to my brother. The lieutenant owed me many favors, so he sent another man. He went to the front and returned with no problems. I don't think my brother knew anything about the incident.

The army never tells you where you are going or what is happening. They only told us to be ready to travel at a certain time. We went to the city of Oryol and waited for additional orders. We had to travel by cargo trains. It was late at night, and we had only one small lamp. When we arrived at Oryol, we had to sit on hard wooden benches in the cold station and wait. We saw many trains full of equipment and soldiers heading towards the front. There were German planes in the area, but they didn't bomb us. We Jews tried to stay together. We were all from the same area in Poland and knew each other.

As we waited, we worried about being put into the army and the front line. The lieutenant and the sergeant were more worried than the rest of us. They had a good time with us and didn't want to leave. Some men from our group jumped onto empty trains that were returning from the front and deserted. A few men had a chance to get away, but a large group of men deserting would be easily caught. The rest of us just waited in that cold station for orders that would determine our future.

After a few days, four of us who were Jewish decided to desert also. We waited for our chance and one night jumped onto an empty train and were gone. We were frozen cold by the train ride and got off the next morning at the town of Lyubertsy. Since we had no papers, we had to go to the army draft headquarters in the town. We had to tell them a story to get a set of identity papers and orders. The police stopped people all the time on the street and checked for deserters. It was impossible to hide.

In the draft station, we saw many other men who had deserted. We were all surprised to see each other. We still had our rifles. Everything was confused in the army draft station. There were many soldiers who had been surrounded by the Germans and had their units destroyed. They were all sent to Lucha when they returned to the Russian lines. It was easy to get lost in the crowd. We just told the authorities that we were lost from our units and were part of the destroyed armies. No one asked any questions. We said we wanted to enlist in the Polish Army.

There was no Polish Army then, but we had heard that the Russians were organizing one deep in Russia. We hoped that if we could get there we would be safe. They put every Pole who volunteered into the Polish Army. We had to wait for three days in the draft station before our orders were approved to join the Polish Army. All the Jews wanted to stay together. It was safer when we were together. There were many anti-Semites who would kill Jews if they had a chance, so we stayed together and helped each other. Many of us knew each other from before the war in Poland. We trusted each other and felt safe together.

They told us to report to the Polish consul, who was about six hundred miles away. We went by train and took our time. We would ride about sixty miles and get off for the night. We spent the nights at the local collectives. When we were in the collectives, we would chop wood, milk the cows, and do other work for the collective. There were no men left. They were all in the army. The women would give us some cabbage soup with a piece of pork. It was good. We were on those trains for more than three weeks. There were no problems for us then because we had orders and were legitimate as far as the government was concerned. We could have made the trip in three or four days, but we took our time.

I had trouble with my teeth while we were going from Lucha to S_____, where the Polish consul was located. I was outside in the cold weather, and the cold was hurting my teeth terribly. My friends left me at the collective and told the manager of the collective to take care of me until I was better. They had to leave the next day to go to the army. It was snowing, and the temperature was bitter cold. I was hungry and only wanted a piece of bread or a potato, but I could not find any food.

I stayed in that collective with tears in my eyes and a broken heart. I lay on top of the oven in the kitchen where it was warm. They had corn up there to dry, and I stayed with the corn. I kept my face on the oven to warm my teeth. I had to return to the village of B_____, where an army station was located, to find help for my teeth. Two men from the collective had to take a part from their tractor to that town to be fixed, and they said they would take me there. I was so sick, I was crying like a baby. I didn't know what to do. I was sure that when the army got hold of me they would put me in the front line, and I would be killed. I would never have a chance. We got only four kilometers from the collective and had to turn back because of the heavy snow. I went back to the top of the stove, and after four days, when the storm was over, my teeth were better. I decided to try to find my friends and join the Polish Army as I had planned to do. I jumped the next train and was soon on my way again. My teeth no longer hurt me.

I soon found my friends and continued my travels. Every night we stopped at a different collective and did some work for the women for our room and some food.

There was a lot of hard work to be done on the collectives, and we helped with whatever we could do.

One of the fellows in the group was named Joseph Flaxman. He was from the city of Lemburg and was a former Polish policeman who had been stationed near my village before the war. He was forty-two years old at the time. We stopped at one collective and stayed with a lady and her two daughters. This fellow married one of the girls, so we decided to stay on for a few days. We were sleeping on the floor of the house and had a good time. I stayed with Flaxman and his new wife, while my brother and Zelkie stayed in another room with another family. After three days, we had to leave the collective. Before we left, we took some extra food from their storage area in front of the house. We took only what we needed and left the rest for the family. I felt bad about doing that, but I was hungry and had no other choice. I had only one pound of bread every day for food, and I needed more to survive.

At eight that morning, after a good breakfast of scrambled eggs, we all left for the train. Flaxman told his new wife that he wanted to go with us to the train. The woman went with us to say goodbye. Flaxman got on the train and continued to talk to us. We put everything we had on the train and waited for it to go. When the train began to start up, he began to shake hands and say goodbye again. The train was moving faster and faster, but Flaxman stayed on the train. He never intended to get off. He left his new wife standing on the station. He was a real thief. He later cheated me of seven hundred fifty rubles, and I was his friend. I would never hurt anyone like he did.

⚐ ⚐

When we finally arrived in S_____, we went right to the Polish consul to report. We found a Russian NKVD [People's Commissariat of Internal Affairs] guard around the building and couldn't get in because we didn't have the proper papers. We had to go back to the Russian army draft station in S_____ and hope for the best. We didn't know what to do. We wanted to get into the Polish Army, where we hoped we would be safe, but the way seemed blocked. The two men who were traveling with us, Pian and Kessler, were holding our papers and had a plan to get by the NKVD. They kept it to themselves and told the rest of us nothing. They could keep good secrets.

When we arrived at the draft station, we saw that it was crowded with men. Pian and Kessler began to cry and scream. They went to the commander and told him that someone had stolen their papers. They told him the truth, except when they said that they had a paper to get into the Polish consul. Of course, we had no such paper. The commander gave us new papers, and we were soon past the NKVD guard and on our way to the Polish Army.

The Polish consul put us on a train and sent us two hundred eighty kilometers further into Russia. It was a cargo train, not a passenger train. There were two Russian women sleeping over me. They were speculators traveling with goods. I jumped up to one of the higher benches and lay down next to them. They didn't like it, but there was nothing they could do about it. Traveling near us were two men. One was an older man, and the other was a young man. They were uncle and nephew. We were all cold, dirty, and hungry on that train. Conditions were very bad. Whenever the train stopped, everyone would run off to relieve themselves and get fresh water in their pails. All the people carried small pails with them for water and food. There were also two small boys on the train, six and eight years old. They were orphans and all alone. I don't know where they were going. We all felt sorry for them and gave them some bread to eat.

The two women would sleep together on the same bench. They had three large suitcases which they covered with a large blanket. It was a good blanket in top shape. I was cold and needed that blanket and began to think about how I could steal it. Sometimes during the night the blanket would fall off the suitcases onto the two men who were sleeping below. They would pass it back to the women. I knew it was wrong to steal, but I really needed that blanket. I lost my home and my family and didn't know what was going to happen to me. I wanted that blanket. They were speculators, and I needed it more than they did. I watched them the next night, and when I saw the blanket fall, I grabbed it and passed it to one of my friends who passed it to another friend on the other side of the train. When the women got up in the morning they began to wash and look for the blanket. Of course it was gone. The women accused the boys of stealing it. The boys had disappeared during the night, and the women decided that they were guilty. They could really curse.

Everyone had to have a pail for food and water on the train. I didn't have a pail at that time. Near the door of the train, I saw a Jew with a Russian woman. They were both dressed very nicely and had expensive clothes. They had an expensive suitcase, and I began to think about how I could steal it. I decided it was too risky, so I began to concentrate on the man's pail. It was porcelain and made very well. I needed a pail and was dying to take it. How could I do it? We were on the train, and it seemed impossible to steal. I decided to make my move when I got off the train. When the train stopped at the station, I started to get off slowly and grabbed the pail as I was stepping down. I ran as fast as I could and was soon lost in the crowd. The woman began to scream at me, but I was soon gone. I really wasn't too worried about them, because I knew they didn't want to get off the train and miss it for a pail. They also looked like speculators, and it might be danger-ous for them to attract too much attention to themselves or go to the police. The police wouldn't be interested in such a small thing.

We went to the local draft station to find out where the Polish Army was located. I waited outside while Pian and Kessler went inside to find the information we needed. While we were standing there, the police came along and asked to see our papers. They wanted to know what business we had in the city. We told them we were on our way to enlist in the Polish Army, and they told us we had to go with them to see the commanding officer of the town. In the war, the Russians put army commanders in charge of the towns instead of mayors. They were always checking your papers.

The commander asked us many questions. We told him we wanted to join the Polish Army. He began to curse at us and was very angry. We were all scared of him. He accused us of shirking our duty and running around Russia while we should be fighting to defeat Hitler. He checked our belongings and took our good shoes. He told Pian and I to go outside and wait for him but kept Kessler with him to question further. He threatened to have us all shot as shirkers. We were very worried because he was an important man and no one to be fooled with. After a few hours, the Russian army commander put us to work loading trucks with apples, oranges, and lemons.

The fruit was in a basement, and we had to carry it up to the trucks. We ate all that we could. We did not know what was going to happen to us or where Kessler was.

There was a restaurant located across the street from where we were working, and we went there for lunch. We had to buy the food with our own money. When we walked into the restaurant we saw Kessler sitting in the rear. We ran to him, and he told us not to worry. He said everything was going to be fine. The commander was Jewish, and he didn't do to us what he had threatened to do. He gave us passes to join the Polish Army, and everything was fine. Kessler told us the Polish Army was located deeper in Middle Asia, and we had to travel further to find it. The commander did us a big favor. I never could find out exactly what Kessler said to him to make him change his mind. In any case, we were very lucky.

We now had to travel to a town not far from the city of Tashkent. It took us seven days to get there. Before we left, we went to the town bath and got clean for the first time in many months. We really needed that bath. We had to take all our clothes off and go into the large room with showers. They gave us some soap, and we had to give our dirty clothes to some women, who cleaned them for us.

There was an old man standing in the corner of the shower room shaking. He had spent many years in Siberia and was in bad shape. Another man there was younger, but was in just as bad shape. He looked like a living ghost. He was a Jewish fellow from Warsaw and had been a noncommissioned officer in the Polish Army before 1939 and had been captured by the Russians. He suffered terribly in a Russian camp and was released when the war started. We all wanted to cry when we saw him. He looked like he had suffered great pain. We helped him wash and did what we could for him. It was hard to believe. He was only a shell of a man and was destroyed by his past experience. We gave him food and some money. I saw many people like that in the war. Some of them survived the war only to die when they got good food and treatment after the war. They had suffered too long and couldn't take the change. It was too much for them. I have no idea what happened to this man.

⩗ ⩘

The Polish Army was located near the town of Lugovoy. It was three days travel from Tashkent, and we had to wait for weeks after we arrived to join the army. No one could bother us because we had the proper papers. We slept in the local train station and could buy food there. We could buy one bowl of soup every day. On some days we managed to sneak two bowls of soup. The soup was made from oil and cabbage, with an occasional piece of pork. It wasn't much, but at least it was hot and something to put in my stomach.

In February 1942, I joined the Polish Army. We felt better when we had Polish officers around us. It was more like home. I was in the Polish Army for three months. My brother couldn't get in because he was sick. My brother and Zelkie went to work in the local collective. I would help him with food whenever I could.

After three months, the army was going to move out. I didn't want to leave my brother, so I decided to leave the army. It was an easy matter to do. All I had to do was to give back the uniform, and I was out of the army.

Now I began to struggle for my life. Life became very difficult for me. I eventually went to a nearby village where I found a countryman of mine who was a shoemaker, and I went to work for him. He just gave me enough food to eat and that was all. I knew nothing about shoes, but I soon learned.

Zelkie and my brother and I found a place to sleep with a man and his nephew. We slept on the floor of the entrance room to a house. It was called the cold room because it was partially open to the outside and was always cold. Zelkie and my brother both had good jobs. They worked as watchmen in the bakery and could steal food. The Polish Army had moved out by this time, and Kessler and Pian left with the army. Only Zelkie and my brother and I decided to stay. Zelkie didn't like the new Russian version of the Polish Army and refused to join.

On May 1, 1942, Zelkie had to say Kaddish [a Jewish hymn of mourning] for his dead father. Late at night I saw the door open and two men come into the cold room. I thought it was the old man coming home from work, so I closed my eyes and tried to go back to sleep. I felt uneasy and opened my eyes again to look at the two men. One man held something that shone in the moonlight. It was a piece of metal. As he raised it over his head, I recognized him as the Ukrainian called Jan. He was thrown out of the Russian Army and was a very bad tempered fellow. He would stop any Jew on the street and rob him on the spot. I knew in an instant that Jan was going to kill us and steal what we had. He was a real murderer. I began to scream, and he stopped, turned around, and ran out of the room. I was lucky I scared him away. We were all awake for the rest of the night.

Life was now a real struggle. I had to look for many kinds of work and went from collective to collective. I just wanted a job where I could have a little to eat. That was the only important thing—just to find enough to eat. I was hungry all the time.

By June, the heat was oppressive. It was still cold at night, and I made good use of the blanket I stole from the women on the train. I was sleeping on the floor with the dirt all the time. I had no underwear and was cold at night. I had body lice and had to go to the cleaning station every other day to get deloused. It was not pleasant. There was really no way to stay clean. I began to get sick and soon became ill with malaria. Now my really difficult time began. I was sick and couldn't work and couldn't get anything to eat because I wasn't working. I had constant diarrhea and sores all over my legs and found it difficult to walk.

I managed to go to the doctor. The doctor was a Jewish woman from Kharkov. She cleaned me up and gave me some medicine to put on my legs. I had to go back every day for treatment to clean my legs. The treatment cost me fifty kopecks, but it was worth it. Gradually I began to feel better. The women in the village showed me how to wash clothes with charcoal. I was still hungry and needed food to get my strength back, but I had none. All I could get to eat was some bread. It wasn't enough, and I suffered from lack of food. I managed to steal a chicken and cook it. I shared it with my brother and Zelkie, and the second day after I ate the chicken, I began to feel better. I sold my blanket to to a Ukrainian woman for four pounds of butter and two quarts of milk and some heavy bread. Then I looked for work at the railroad station.

I met a man at the station named Alexi. Alexi needed a strong man to help him with his horses. He had a woman helping him, but she couldn't handle them. One horse was blind in one eye and had a bad disposition. He never wanted to pull the wagon. The other horse was young and needed to be trained. I had a bit stick and soon had the situation under control, though I had to stay away from the big horse because he would always try to kick me. Alexi had a wagon and had to haul goods from the station. He was under pressure from the government to work hard. They could always put him in the army and give his job to another man. It was a good job, and many people wanted to have it. He was happy to have me work for him.

I was with him from July 1942 until July 1943. I remember Alexi very well. He was a good man, and he didn't want me to leave. He used to cook food in his office, and I had enough to eat. It was a mistake when I left him. I was sorry later.

Chapter Eight

The Director

Everything in the village was controlled by the Russian government. Even the smallest shoemaker worked for the government. Most of the things the people needed, they had to barter for with another person. Every item for sale in the village was old and used. We repaired what we had or did without. It was impossible to buy anything new, especially clothing. There were very few young people in the village. All of the men were in the army, and many of the young girls went to the cities to work in the large factories doing war work. The remaining people in the village were mostly women, children, and old people. Everyone in that village suffered because of the war. Everyone had a sad story to tell.

I remember one woman and a child very much. Her husband was a doctor and was serving with the army. She slept in a little room with her son, and she had a small stove to keep warm when she could find some coal for it to burn. She cooked wheat in water to make soup. That was all she had to eat. She was sick and couldn't work. She had a hard time, and I tried to help her with some food when I was able to get some extra to eat. The government rationed food and allowed adults just one pound of bread a day and children just three hundred grams a day. Many people died from hunger and malnutrition. It was a terrible time. If you had anything to eat, you had to eat it quickly or else hide it before someone saw it.

There was a sugar factory in the village. The people who worked in that factory were lucky. They could steal sugar and sell it for extra food, so at least they could survive the hunger. There was also a public restaurant located near the railroad station. It was a big place, and I got to know the people who worked there. I used to deliver coal to the restaurant every day. They always needed a lot of coal because they were open twenty-four hours a day. I had a deal with the cook. I would see that they got good quality coal, and he would give me some hot food to eat. Everyone who worked in the restaurant stole food. People worked there just for the food and received no money. There were many jobs like that in Russia during the war, and everyone was happy to work for food. Many times that was the only way you could eat.

People would come to the restaurant to beg for food. They would wait for the garbage and search for scraped-off food in the garbage cans. Everyone in the village needed more food. We had mainly bread and potatoes to eat, and no vegetables, meat, or fat. This was how people lived.

I was happy because I felt I was safe from the Russian Army. I wanted to survive the war and knew I had to stay out of the army and away from the fighting. As long as I had my papers and a job, I was safe.

My brother was with me, and he met a watchman who guarded the cattle of the local collective. The collective let the cattle stay out at night to graze and needed a man to watch them. That was the best job to have. You could work at night and do your own business during the day. The watchman would also sleep at night while he was supposed to look after the cattle. The collective paid him with food, not money. Whatever the collective had to eat, the watchman had to eat. Sometimes he had bread with sugar and butter, and he would milk some of the cows at night and drink the milk or sell it in the town. No one would ever know.

The watchman, a fellow named Michael from Poland, and my brother got together and decided to steal a cow from the collective and slaughter it. They would split the profit and sell the meat in the town. It was easy to sell the meat because the government never had meat for the people in the village. The town people would pay well for a piece of meat. I was working for the Director and knew nothing of the plan.

They slaughtered the cow and began to sell the meat. The Russian Jews in the village had some money to pay for the meat. They had had time to take many of their possessions with them after the start of the war. Many of them also had good jobs. At the same time that my brother slaughtered his cow, another man in the village from Poland named Feliks also stole a cow and slaughtered it. That cow belonged to one of the villagers, who kept it in a barn behind his house. He needed it to give milk to his children. The next morning, when the man came out to milk his cow, he saw the bloody remains. We could never understand how Feliks slaughtered the cow without being heard. The man had a guard dog, and the animal never made a sound. When I got up, I saw that there was a great disturbance in the village. The Russian militia was called in to solve the crime. The Russians suspected the Poles, but there was no proof of who was responsible. Only many years later did I learn that Feliks was the man who killed the villager's cow. Feliks was long gone by morning and never returned. My brother and Michael had slaughtered their cow at the collective and knew nothing of what had happened in the village.

There were two sisters who lived in the village, Alisa and Elena. Elena was married and had a young son. Her husband was in the army and had been away from home since the start of the war. My brother and Michael spent many hours over at their house having a good time. They were speculators and sold whatever they could on the black market. They had flour, shoes, and clothes to sell in their house. My brother and Michael carried the cow's meat to Elena's house to sell. They arrived at the house early in the morning, and Michael left while my brother stayed in the house and went to sleep.

When the morning came, the watchman got off work and began to walk into the town with the skin. He could sell it to make leather and make a lot of money. There was only one man in the village that had the skill necessary to do the work, so the watchman was going to his house. By the time he arrived in the village, everyone was running around looking for the man who had slaughtered the cow in the village. The watchman was stopped almost at once by the militia and had to show them his package. It wasn't the skin of the villager's cow, but they wanted to know what he was doing with the skin of another slaughtered cow. He had no business with it. It didn't belong to him. He was caught red-handed and arrested by the militia.

A group of villagers quickly gathered around the watchman in an angry mood. The militia made him tell them where the rest of the cow was, and they all began to march to Elena's house, where my brother was sleeping. My brother woke up just before they arrived, looked out the window, and saw the militia escorting the watchman, who was carrying the skin to the house. Following the watchman was a large group of villagers yelling and screaming threats. It was too late to run from the house, and my brother was trapped. Michael had already left and was safe, but my brother knew he was caught unless he did some fast thinking. My brother took a scarf and covered his head and hid in a corner of the house. Everyone came into the house and filled the room with people. My brother mixed in among the villagers and managed to get away while the militia was questioning the watchman. No one saw him or heard him leave. He was very lucky. The watchman served five years in a work camp and had a hard time. The Russians were always hard on anyone who was convicted of an economic crime.

Zelkie came to my room and told me the whole story. The militia was looking for my brother and Michael. Elena's boy came to see me and asked where my brother was. The militia had arrested his mother, and he wanted a place to sleep. He had no place to go.

I was surprised to hear what had happened, but happy to learn of my brother's escape. I knew my brother wasn't working and was up to no good, but I had no idea he was stealing cattle. I was sick with worry for my brother and walked around the village looking for him. The whole village was talking about the incident. The Russians were very angry at the Poles in the village and believed they were all up to no good. I wanted to help my brother, but I couldn't find him.

After I returned home from work that night, I saw two boys waiting for me. I used to give them food on occasion, and they were my friends. They told me that my brother and Michael were hiding with them. They wanted to go to the city of J_____. They could not take the train because the militia was watching the trains. They had to walk and would follow the railroad track so they wouldn't get lost. I went to see my brother and took him everything I could get my hands on. I took all my food and money for him. I gave him everything. He was crying and said he didn't know what was going to happen to him. I was angry with him. He could have come with me and worked for the Director, but that was not good enough for him. He had to be a big man, and now he was in trouble with the authorities. I felt sad when I left him. I had lost my entire family, and I didn't know if I would ever see him again. For six weeks after he left, I had no information from him. Everything began to quiet down in the village. The militia told the man who owned the cow that the two other men responsible for the theft had fled. They never found out that Felki was really responsible.

Six weeks later, I heard someone knocking on my window. The man told me he had to talk to me. His name was Kessler, and I knew him from Poland before the war. He was from the town of Radymno, which was located about sixty kilometers from my home village. He was a Polish policeman before the war and was one of the first to flee from the Germans. The Germans always killed the Polish police first.

I later found out that when my brother arrived in J_____ he walked around for a few days looking for help. There were many Polish Jews in J_____, and my brother persuaded one of them, a tailor, to hide him in his cellar. My brother had to get off the street because of the danger of the police. The Russian police always stopped people to check papers. You never knew when you would be stopped. My brother hid in the cellar under the floor of the kitchen for six weeks. The old man shared his food with my brother and was good to him. It was not enough to eat, but it was something.

I knew Kessler when I was in the Polish army. He told me how my brother was doing in J_____ and said my brother needed help and would take any food or money I had to him. I gave him everything I could find. He took my food and a blanket, as well as a large amount of money.

The next week my brother returned from J_____. He said he had to leave because he had no way to stay there any longer. Kessler had run off with everything and had not given my brother any of the things I sent for him. That was a terrible thing to do. I had my brother in my room for a few days. After a week, I returned from work to find that he was gone. Zelkie told me that he decided to go back and live with Alisa and Elena, who were out of jail by this time. I was worried that the militia would find him and arrest him. He took a terrible chance in exposing himself in the village. My brother returned later that night and told me not to worry; everything was fixed up with the militia. In a few days he was back to his old ways. He was very lucky to escape. The watchman had to serve five years in jail and had a hard time. I saw the watchman in the refugee camp in Austria after the war. He told me that it was very rough in jail, and he suffered greatly.

The Director was in charge of the local railroad station, and my job was to take care of his horses and do the hauling. There were about fifteen trains a day that stopped at the station. Many people were so tired and hungry when they got off the trains that they collapsed on the station floor. I had to help them. I had free boiled water for everyone. With a little tea and sugar, the people had a good drink. I supplied only the water, not the tea or sugar.

One of my main jobs for the Director was to deliver coal from the station to various places in the village. Wagons loaded with potatoes from the local collective would travel the same roads I did with the coal. Sometimes potatoes would fall from the wagons. The drivers would never stop to pick them up, and they would just remain on the dirt road. I would always look for these potatoes because they were on the ground and would only rot.

I unloaded some coal for the police one day, and they saw my bag of potatoes. They asked me where I got them, and I told them the truth: I found them on the road. The police took the potatoes away from me and made me come into the station. They asked me all kinds of questions and made me sign a document. I thought I was in a lot of trouble. They told me that the potatoes were government property, and I was not to touch them even if they were on the ground. I had to wait several hours in the station while they continued to question me. My horse was tied up outside the station, and I forgot all about him. He managed to get loose and walked back to his stall, where the Director saw him. He thought I was hurt and began to look for me. Later that night the police let me go and told me to report back in the morning. I found the Director and told him the whole story. He told me not to worry and said he would go to the police and take care of everything. The next morning he saw the police and settled the whole matter for me. It was a good lesson for me. You could get in trouble with the Russian police for no reason at all. I was very careful after that time.

Every morning I heard the latest war news. There were some loudspeakers in the village that we listened to. The Russians told us about the war, and that the Germans were killing the Jews and many other people. I just couldn't believe it. I hoped my family was safe in the woods, but I had my doubts.

I was with the Director for over one year. I eventually decided to leave him. I was getting tired of delivering coal and wanted a change. I was afraid that if I stayed too long, the Russians would keep me there after the war, and I would never get back home to see my family.

I decided to leave the village and join the Polish Army again. The Director begged me not to leave, but I would not listen to him. I was a fool and made a bad mistake when I left. I had a bad time right from the start. While I was waiting at the station for the train to take me to the Polish Army, I had my head on my bag, which I filled with tea to sell for food along the way. During the night I felt my head sinking lower and lower. The man behind me had cut a hole in the bag and was stealing my tea. I jumped up and began to kick him, but he ran away with my tea.

When the train came the next morning it was full of people. I threw my bag in an open window and began to climb into the car. It was too full of people, and I couldn't get in. While I was struggling to get in, a man grabbed my wallet and ran away. I jumped down and the train began to pull away with my bag inside. I lost all my money and belongings. I should have stayed with the Director. My life after that morning was hard, and I was sorry I ever left.

Chapter Nine

The Work Camp

After I said goodbye to the Director, I took a train to find the Polish Army. Many Jews on the train wanted to join the Polish Army also. It took about two weeks to find the army. The Army was located at a camp about one hundred miles south of Moscow. There were about thirteen hundred men on the train by the time we arrived at the army camp. During the train ride, people would stop us at the stations and ask for any news we had about the war. This was the only way they could find information other than what the government told them. We always exchanged information freely. You had to talk to someone who came from another section of the country to find out what was happening there. We also had many accidents on the train during the trip. The cars were always full of men who were drunk and rowdy. Sometimes a man would fall off the train or fall between the cars and be killed.

There were many bomb craters near the Polish Army camp. German planes would fly over from time to time and bomb the Poles. The planes caused little damage, and the soldiers did not seem to be worried about them. We had to walk several kilometers from the train station to the army. When we arrived at the headquarters, we saw that only Russian officers were in charge. There were no Polish officers. It was a Polish army with Russian officers. The Russians did not trust the Poles. I thought it was going to be the same as the old Polish Army I served in before I left home; I was a fool. Many other men were also discouraged and decided not to join the army. They couldn't keep us, so we just walked back to the train and climbed on for the return trip. About six hundred of us decided to return.

I knew now that I had made a mistake, and I hoped I could get back to the Director and my good job. I only wanted to get there safely. I had no papers or reason to be on the train, and I could be picked up by the Russian police at any time. During the trip, many of the men began to steal things from other trains and people at the railroad stations. The people who were in charge of the train saw what was happening but said nothing. The Russian officer in charge of the train was very angry with us. We had traveled several hundred miles to join the Polish Army and then refused to join. We were now making further problems for the people who ran the trains. Unknown to us, the Russian officer called ahead to the next station for NKVD troops to meet the trains. This station was close to my destination, and my heart sank when we pulled into the station and saw the troops. I knew I would never see the Director again. The troops ordered us all off the train and told us we were under arrest. They took us under guard on another train to the city of Abdulino, several hundred miles to the east. There was a Russian work camp located there, and they put us in the camp.

The camp was a big affair. It had at least twenty thousand people and many large buildings. There was a high, electrical double fence separated by a ten-foot strip of finely-raked dirt that went around the camp. The dirt was checked every day for footprints and then raked over again. It was impossible to escape from the camp. Even if you could get through the wire, no prisoner could get far. The police constantly stopped people near the camp and checked their papers. Without the proper papers, they would pick you up immediately.

Most of the people who worked in the camp were in trouble with the government. Many had broken the law and had to serve five or ten years. Many others were like me. I was in the camp because I refused to join the Polish Army. I had no purpose or function as far as the government was concerned. I was just loose and wandering around the country. Worst of all, I wasn't working. The NKVD just took me off the train and put me in the camp. I guess the government needed more people to work in the camp, and we were available. I was not convicted of any crime, but I was in the camp just the same. I had to work there until they told me I could leave. I had no sentence, so technically I was not a prisoner.

Everything was a secret in the camp. We weren't supposed to know what was made in the various buildings, but I soon found out that the camp made tanks. Soon after I arrived in the camp, I was told I was going to be there for a long time. They asked what my profession was before the war. I told them I was a butcher, and since they had no use for a butcher, they put me to work in a warehouse. I didn't really care.

Working in a warehouse turned out to be a good job. I had a chance to steal from the warehouse and buy what I needed to survive in the camp. It took me a few weeks to learn my way around the camp, but I was soon settled in. I was paid in food stamps by the manager of the warehouse. Everyone in the camp received food stamps. There was no money, only food. I was hungry all the time and really didn't need money, but I did need the food. What was important was to have a job where you could steal some food. Everyone was hungry. Sometimes when a truck would come into the camp and go to the warehouse, people would rush the truck and steal as much as they could carry. They ran away and were soon lost in the crowd. What could we do? Everyone was hungry and had to steal.

I always got up for work at five in the morning. I was hungry but had nothing to eat except some boiled water. I had a ration card for seven hundred grams of bread a day. That wasn't enough to eat, so I spent a good deal of my time trying to get more food. Some days the snow was so deep in the camp that I didn't go to the restaurant for dinner. I always tried to keep some extra food with me for such an emergency. The tickets were always good, and I would go the next day and take two meals. My boss always had extra food in his desk, which he would eat when he thought we were not looking. I knew he was stealing a lot from the government because his food was very expensive, and he couldn't afford it on just his salary. He had butter, white bread, and goat's milk. He always had extra food to take to his family, who lived in a nearby town. He wasn't a prisoner but was a Party man and had a good job running the warehouse.

My ear was very sore soon after I arrived in the camp. It began to bother me all the time, and I had no way to get medical attention for it. I thought it was sore from the constant cold or the camp, so I began to put cotton in my ears to protect them. In the morning I would take the old cotton out of my ears and put in fresh cotton. Within a few weeks, I had a constant ringing in my ears. I paid no attention to the ringing because it wasn't too loud. It was there all the time. Finally it became so bad I knew I had to get help. I asked the manager to send me to the doctor in the town. He gave me permission, and I walked to the town with a soldier. I went to the clinic and told the woman doctor of my ear problem. She took a metal probe, poled in my ear, and then took a pair of tweezers, put them in my ear, and pulled out a large wad of old cotton. The moment it was out I felt better. It was as if I had been deaf for months. The cotton smelled terrible. She cleaned out my ear with a solution, and I felt much better. I believe she saved my life. That ringing in my ear was driving me crazy.

Every four months we had to take inventory in the warehouse. It usually took two days for us to count everything, and the warehouse was always short. I was always stealing what I could, and the other men in the warehouse did the same. Once I took a package of tea and managed to sell it to someone from the town for eleven hundred rubles. That was a lot of money, considering that the manager of the warehouse made only one hundred and eighty rubles a month.

After a few months, my boss decided to leave and get another job because he was afraid that the government would blame him for the inventory shortages. The man who replaced him was a wounded soldier who lived in the town. He was smarter than the first manager, but I still managed to steal what I needed. I was very careful and would always wait for my chance. He couldn't watch me all the time. I planned everything in advance and was never caught.

Once we received a shipment of blankets and rubber boots. We had to count everything to prevent stealing, and while I was counting the boots I was thinking how I could steal a pair. By the time we finished counting the shipment, it was six at night and time to go home. Two Russian women had accompanied the shipment from the factory and were responsible for it. They decided to sleep in the warehouse with the boots and blankets until all the papers were signed the next morning. The manager asked me and another man to stay in the warehouse and watch the women. He locked the building for the night with the four of us inside watching each other. The women were honest, but we two men were thinking of how best to steal some boots. The man who stayed with me was supposed to leave the camp the next day to travel two hundred kilometers to a collective to get butter for the camp. The trip took several days, and he had to ride in the back of an open truck over some terrible roads. It was a terrible job, and I never wanted to do it. The Russian man wanted to fill his pockets with loose tea to sell outside of the camp. I pretended not to see his stealing the tea. It was his business. I would wait my turn for the boots. He filled his pockets and waited for the morning. He took four bags of soap also. The women heard us talking during the night and became suspicious of us. They sensed we were up to no good.

At eight that morning, the door of the warehouse opened up, and the boss came in to see us. He went first to the women who told him they suspected us of stealing from the warehouse. He knew the other man had to leave first thing in the morning and suspected him. He was a Russian and did not want to get another Russian in trouble. Still, he had to check us for stealing. The women reported us, and he had no choice. He called me over first and checked my pockets. Of course, I was clean. I had to work that day and would only do my stealing at night. It was foolish to steal something in the morning and to carry it around all day. That was a sure way to be caught. While I was being checked, my friend managed to get rid of his soap. The tea was another matter. He tried to dump it from his pockets, but much of it was sticking to the inside lining. It was all loose in his pockets. The manager found the tea in his pockets and said nothing. If he reported him for stealing, he would be in serious trouble. The man left to get the butter.

Later that day, I managed to sneak a large pair of rubber boots out of the warehouse under my coat. I hid the boots and sold them to a man in town several weeks later. I also managed to steal some soap. I would trade with people who came up to the wire of the camp from the town. I would show them what I had and would arrange a price and slip the goods through the wire. Once a year all the people of the camp were given new underwear, and I would trade that also. I was full of lice, and it made no sense putting on clean underwear. It would only be full of lice in a few days. It was much better to trade it for some food I could eat. Sometimes I would cheat the person I was trading with through the fence. I would put my goods in some paper and show them to a buyer. While he decided, I put the paper back in my coat. When the deal was made, I gave out another package and ran away. Everything had to be done quickly through the wire. It was strictly illegal to exchange anything in that manner, and the guards were constantly looking for such activities. I never felt bad about that. I was in that camp and had nothing and had to survive by using my brains. I stole only what I needed to survive and tried never to really hurt another person.

☒ ☒

I knew that my time in the warehouse was growing short. The new manager wanted to replace us with new people from the town. He knew we were stealing but could not catch us. He also had many relatives who needed jobs, and that was good work. He told us that his sister was going to come to work with us, and I was fired. I would have to find another job in the camp.

I had to get out of that camp. I was in that camp from July 1943 until October 1944. I was lucky so far, but I could not count on my luck holding out. I could get hurt or sick and that was no place to be. It was also too easy to get into trouble there, and I could be in jail for years for doing nothing. I just had to find a way to get out.

I had a letter from my cousin (who is now in Israel) during the time I was in the camp. He was working on a collective and said that if I could reach him, he would find me a job on the collective, and I could be with him. I was lonely and wanted to be with him. I missed my family and longed to see my cousin again. People are different in Europe than they are here [in the U.S.]. When a European meets a person from his village or local area, he feels like he has met his brother. Friends and family are very important. In Europe, families always stayed together. Children remained home until they were married. They stayed with their parents no matter how old they were. When they were married, they left and set up another house a few doors away. Families always wanted to be close in Europe. It was important to them.

I had no idea of when the war would end. I didn't know what I was going to do after the war. Everything was uncertain. I had no plans for the future. The war had destroyed everything. Everyone in Russia waited for the government to tell them what to do. The war had lasted for four years and seemed like an eternity to me. I never heard of a war lasting that long.

I began to think of how I could get out of that camp. After all, I had committed no crime, so I should be able to get out, but I had to have a reason to leave. What could I use for my reason to leave the camp? My real reason was personal. I wanted to find my cousin, but I couldn't tell the Russians that. They would never let me go. I had to find a reason they would accept.

I heard that the Russians were still recruiting Poles to join the Polish Army. I bribed a man and got permission to join the Polish Army – again! Soon after I had permission to join the army, I heard that the Russians were recruiting woodcutters in the camp to cut wood near Moscow. I thought matters over and decided to join the woodcutters. After all, I might fail to escape from the army train, and, in case of failure, it was better to cut wood than to fight in the army. The latter was hard work, but it wouldn't kill me. And that was how I left the camp.

Chapter Ten

I Find My Cousin

There were many different types of men on the train to cut wood. One man was a former manager of a large collective. He was caught stealing from the collective and was sent to the camp. He was an older man in his sixties and was very cunning. The train had to stop at many stations, and he was always trying to steal something. I got off the train with him at one station and followed him to a peasant's food stand. It was a cold day, and he ordered two glasses of vodka and some pickles from the woman. I thought he was treating me to the food. I was wrong. The woman asked me for the money, and when I turned, I found the former manager was gone. He ordered the food and left me to pay for it. I told her I didn't order the food, but my friend had ordered it and said she should get her money from him. She was angry and began to curse at me. I could see him on the train laughing at me. He thought it was all very funny. I just left her and gave her no money. I felt bad about the matter, but I had not ordered the food and saw no reason to pay for it.

Sometimes the train would wait for two or three days in a station for the tracks to clear. We arrived at one station late at night and had to wait until morning, so we went into the station building to spend the night. The floor was covered with people who were trying to keep warm and sleep. The manager told me to start checking all the packages of the sleeping people to see if there was anything we could steal. I started from one side of the room, and he started from the other side. I walked slowly and touched each package with my feet to see what was inside. Many of the people in the station were illegal. They were speculators who were buying and selling goods in violation of the law. We saw one man who was sleeping in the middle of the floor with a promising package and decided to steal it. He was sleeping on it, so I had to get him to move so my friend could grab it. It was very easy to do. I just sat down next to him and told him to move over so I could have room to stretch out. When he moved, my friend grabbed his bag and ran out the front door. It was dark, and the man was tired. By the time he realized what had happened, my friend was gone. He had no idea where to look for his bag. I told him I didn't see anything and that I was tired and going to sleep. I'm sure he was a speculator because he didn't call the police. He didn't want to attract attention to himself. I never did find out what was in that package. The manager kept it all for himself.

The train passed within ten kilometers of my cousin's collective at Eulenburg, and I knew just where I had to get off. My problem was how to get off the train and make the authorities believe I had missed the train by accident. Once I left the train, I had no papers and could be picked up by the police. If the police found me, I could be put back into another camp and sent into the army. I had to make my plans and be sure not to make any mistakes. I did not want to wind up in a worse situation than I was trying to get away from.

The train was guarded by NKVD troops who watched us constantly. I saw that the weak point in their security system was when they let us off the train at the stations to buy food. We always had the soldiers with us, but there was a chance to run.

I waited through the night for the train to stop at Eulenburg so I could make my break. I was very tired and could hardly keep awake, because I had been traveling a long time and needed sleep. I tried not to sleep, but I fell asleep anyway. When I woke up the next morning, I found out that I had missed my stop. I slept right through Eulenburg. I felt sure that I had missed my only chance to get to my cousin, and I was now on my way to cut wood near Moscow. After all my plans, one mistake and I was ruined.

While I was sitting on the floor of the car wondering what to do, the train stopped at another station. I was over twenty miles from Eulenburg, but I had a chance. I had to get off here or else forget about my plans. Many women came up to the train to sell food, and I asked a soldier to go with me so I could buy some fresh milk and bread. He agreed, and we got off the train and walked over to the women. I left all my personal belongings on the train on purpose. I did not want to arouse suspicion, and I wanted to be sure they thought I missed the train by accident. I walked slowly to the women, hoping the train would begin to pull out. You could never tell how long the train would stay in the station. Sometimes it stayed for a few minutes; sometimes it stayed for days. My only chance was if the train was going to leave immediately. I purchased the milk and had the woman put it in my pail. I started to drink it when I heard the train whistle blow once. That was the signal to get back on the train. I started to walk back to the train and heard the second whistle. The train was now starting to move. The soldier ran ahead and jumped on the car and turned to me. He was yelling at me to hurry. I began to run, but slowly because I didn't want to spill the milk. At least that is what I wanted them to think. By the time the third whistle blew, I was close to the fast-moving train, and just as I was about to get on, I tripped on purpose. By the time I got up, the train was out of the station, and the soldier was yelling at me to wait at the station for the next train and to catch them at the next station. I nodded yes and went back to the station. I was sure I made them believe I missed the train by accident, but I missed that train on purpose and had no intention of catching up with them. I wanted to go back to Eulenburg, which was in the opposite direction, and find my cousin.

I now had to decide how to get to my cousin and not be picked up by the police. I talked to the woman who sold me the milk and told her I missed my train. Many people missed trains in Russia, and she said I could go home with her to wait for the train to Eulenburg, which passed through the station later that afternoon. I was very happy to go with her because it was only nine in the morning, and I didn't want to wait until the late afternoon in that station. She said her husband worked for the railroad, and he would help me get to Eulenburg. I went to the house with her and sat down in her hallway. She had her mother living with her, and the old lady kept asking me questions. I tried to be polite to her but not answer her questions. I didn't like to answer so many questions. Her husband came home for lunch, and I talked to him. I gave him some tobacco I had with me, and he was happy to help me. He said the train to Eulenburg passed through the station at four in the afternoon, and he would see that I was on the train.

My cousin told me that people from the collective came to Eulenburg at five in the evening every day to empty their garbage and that if I could get there by five, I could get a ride to the collective with them. I thought I might just have enough time to make it. I caught the train on time and arrived at Eulenburg in a little over a half hour. I got off the train before it came into the station and began to look for the dump. It wasn't easy to find, and I had to be careful who I asked for directions. I wanted to be sure I didn't stop a policeman and ask him for directions. He would ask for my identity papers, and I would be caught. It was freezing cold, and I began to suffer from the temperature. I found out where the dump was, but decided not to take the shortcut through town. I walked around the town to avoid people. The dump was located about one kilometer outside the city on the opposite side from where I jumped off the train. When I arrived at the dump, I saw that it was empty. I stopped an old man who was near me and asked where the trucks for the collective were. He said I just missed them. Now I had a problem.

It was getting dark, and I had no place to stay. It was too dangerous to remain in the town. I had to get to the collective and my cousin before the police saw me. I had to walk; there was no other choice. I was lucky because the old man knew where the collective was, and he gave me good directions. He told me to be careful because there was a concentration camp for political prisoners located near the collective, and I wanted to be sure not to mistake it for the collective. There were guards with dogs all around the camp, so I had to be careful not to go too close to it.

I followed his directions. I walked near the telephone poles so I wouldn't get lost. The ground was deep with snow and ice, and I made a lot of noise as my feet broke through the ice. I walked for four hours before I managed to cover the eighteen kilometers to the collective. I was so cold I ran part of the way to get warm.

Finally, by nine that night, I saw a few houses and went up to them. A man with a rifle came up to me and asked me what my business was. I told him I was looking for my cousin, Joseph Lusky. He knew my cousin well and gave me directions to his house. I had to walk through the woods and across a bridge. My cousin's house had one room and three windows and was on the right after the bridge.

I walked slowly to the house. I was wet and tired. All the windows of the house were frosted up, but through a small hole, I could see my cousin and his wife by the fire. They were eating dinner from one pot with some bread and potatoes. I knocked on the door and my cousin answered the door. At first he didn't recognize me. He had no way to know when I was coming, and I really looked terrible after my ordeal. His wife didn't know me at all. She was from the collective, and her first husband had been killed in the war. She had also lost two children to starvation.

My cousin and I hugged each other and started to cry. We were so happy to see each other. I could not stop talking. I sat down by the table, and he took off my clothes and gave me some food to eat. They began to wash my clothes at once. I was full of lice, and they wanted to be sure I didn't get any in the house. The next day I went to the steam bath in the collective and got rid of all my lice. My cousin said he would talk to the manager of the collective and get me a job. I was happy to see my cousin, and I had made it after all. All my plans had worked, and now I was successful.

The next day my cousin and his wife went to work. I stayed in the house to rest. I waited for ten days for the manager to give me a job. He was afraid to help me because I had no papers. I was illegal, and he was afraid to take a chance. He was a Party man and didn't want any trouble. If I wanted to stay in the collective, I had to get a set of papers. Then he could help me. For the next ten days I had to be careful not to be stopped by the police because without papers I could be arrested and sent to jail or the army. I could not work until I had papers, so I just remained quiet and out of sight.

Chapter Eleven

I Survive the War

The NKVD checked the collective at least twice every week. They were looking for army deserters and people without papers. Everyone had to work to support the war effort. Many people wanted to do their own work and avoided the NKVD. Some turned to crime and robbed houses. They didn't find very much because no one had anything. All the people were poor. Russia was not like the United States, where everyone has some valuables. We were all poor and just trying to survive the war.

The NKVD was looking for men to send into the army. The casualties were enormous, and there was a constant need for men to fill the ranks. Only the most important men in the collective were safe from the army. These were usually the mechanics and blacksmiths, whose labor was needed to keep the collective running. They had a special draft-exempt status from the army and could not be touched by the NKVD. Everyone else could be picked up and put into the army. The NKVD always stopped people to check their papers, and everything had to be in order or you would be in trouble.

After ten days at the collective, I decided to go back to Eulenburg. I left on a cold, snowy day at nine in the morning. I had to walk that whole distance again. I was hiding from the NKVD and had to get a set of papers and find a place for myself. I knew a man who lived in Eulenburg. He was from Luninets in Poland, and I met him in central Russia in 1942. He was traveling around Russia at that time speculating, and I talked with him for a time. He gave me his address and told me to see him if I was ever in the area. He was a speculator and made his living selling pants and old shoes.

I had two thousand four hundred rubles and decided to see him and find out if he could help me buy a set of papers. It wasn't a lot of money, but I hoped it would be enough. If you had enough money, you could buy anything. There were many wounded army men in the town, and they were always willing to sell their papers, but you had to check to be sure that the age and description were right. All the army men had to do was to tell the authorities they lost their papers, and they would get a new set. I hoped the speculator could help me buy a set of papers. Once I had papers, I could return to the collective with my cousin and find a safe job.

I found my friend quickly enough and explained my problem to him. He said he could help me and told me to wait for him in the marketplace. There were many people there, and he said I wouldn't be noticed by the NKVD. I waited there all day in the bitter cold. By six that night he returned and told me he had found me a set of papers, but the soldier wanted six thousand rubles for them. I didn't have half that amount of money and asked him to try to get a better price for me, but the soldier refused to take anything less than six thousand rubles.

I had no papers. I decided the only thing for me to do was to report to the army draft station, tell them a story, and hope they would believe me. I was taking a big chance, but I had no choice. I had no place to stay and no work and no papers and would be caught by the NKVD. It was better to report in than to wait to be caught. I could tell a good story, and perhaps they would believe it. My stories worked before, and I hoped one would work again.

The draft station was closed for the night, and I didn't have a place to stay. It was dangerous to be out on the street. I had to find a room for the night, so I asked my friend if I could stay with him. He lived with an old woman in a big house and had enough room. I didn't need a bed or anything special. I only needed a place to get in from the wind and the cold and away from the NKVD on the streets. My friend made me wait in the doorway for an hour while he asked the old woman if I could stay with them. He returned and told me it was fine, but I would have to pay her five rubles. Then he made me wait another hour while he went on his own business and returned by eight that night. When we got to the house, the old woman wanted ten rubles for the night, and I paid her. I needed a place and would have given her fifty rubles. I slept on the floor by the door. It was cold, but at least I had protection from the wind and a roof over my head.

The next morning I reported to the army draft station. I had no idea what my future held. I told them a real story. I was going to the Polish Army and had missed my train. All my papers and possessions were on the train. The Russian lieutenant was very busy and didn't really pay close attention to me or my story. He gave me a ration card for food for ten days and told me to wait on a bench. I waited there for three days. I had bread and cabbage soup twice a day. The bench was warm, and I was reasonably happy. After a few days, I began to look around and got a part-time job helping in the kitchen. Now I was warm and had enough food to eat, but I needed to find a job.

I had a number from the draft station and could come and go as I wanted to. It was very easy to run away, but I had no place to go and had to stay put until the army decided what to do with me. I was taking a terrible chance being there. They could put me to work in a camp or send me into the army to fight on the front line. There was no way to be sure of my future. My fate was in their hands.

One day I heard the officer in charge of the station talking to a Russian man in a large fur hat. The man told the officer he needed some men to help him in his sugar factory. I jumped up and asked to help him in the factory. I was assigned to the job and was told to wait until I was called. I was happy because that was a good job to have in wartime. Sugar was very valuable, and the work was not hard. You could easily sell sugar and use the money to buy more food. Sugar was just as good as gold. Everyone had a sweet tooth and wanted to buy sugar.

I waited four days on the bench, but the man never returned for me. After a few more days, a woman came into the station and told the officer she needed men to work in her slaughterhouse. Since I was registered to work as a butcher, they called me at once. I ran to the officer and told him I was supposed to work in the sugar factory, but he waved me aside. He said the slaughterhouse was a good place to work, and I really had no choice and had to go work there anyway.

I went with five other men and the woman to the slaughterhouse. There was only one small stove in the middle of the room, and it was not enough to keep us warm. We were told to sleep there for the night and be ready to work in the morning.

I started to work there the next morning. We had a long day from eight in the morning until twelve at night.

We were given an hour for lunch, but since it took at least fifteen minutes to walk to the restaurant, we didn't go too often. In the slaughterhouse was a small room with a stove, and some of the women would cook for everyone who worked there. We killed about one hundred animals every day. We slaughtered cows, goats, lambs, and hogs. All of the meat went to the army. Nothing was sent to the town for the civilian population. There was a large wooden fence around the slaughterhouse to keep out the many thieves who would try to steal some meat. They had no choice, really, because that was the only way to get meat. It was impossible to buy any meat from the government.

One of my jobs was to carry the frozen meat from the freezers to the waiting trucks. One cold day, I slipped while carrying a frozen carcass and dropped it on my large toe. It hurt me a great deal, and I had trouble walking. I was in constant pain from that accident. I still had to work and could not see a doctor. You really had to be hurt before you could see a doctor. I was in bad shape. I was cold all the time and in pain, but I had to work. They were short of help and would take no excuses. Many times the police would drop off convicted criminals to work in the slaughterhouse. I had to work with them and show them what to do.

One day I saw a girl cut off a piece of fat from the tail area. It was good fat and very desirable to cook with. It was also very expensive and sold for one hundred eighty rubles a pound. She had a sharp knife and would cut it from the lamb while it was hanging from the iron hook in the freezer. I didn't want to tell the authorities about it. I only wanted to borrow the knife to cut some fat for myself. She gave me her knife, and I went into the freezer to cut the fat. I was careless and cut my hand instead of the fat. The blood started to shoot from my hand. I ran to the office and told them I cut my hand on the iron hook. It was possible, and they believed me. They had some iodine and bandages in the office, and they fixed me up for a while and told me I had to go to the doctor. I had a deep cut and had to have it sewed up. I lost a lot of blood and had to walk to the doctor. It was nine in the morning and very cold outside.

The doctor's office was in his house, and the waiting room was his front porch. The porch was full of women who were waiting to see the doctor. I was tired from the walk and sat down on a bench to wait for my turn. I was shaking, and my hand was full of blood. The women felt sorry for me and told the doctor to see me at once. He was an old man in his seventies, tall with large white whiskers. He put me in a chair and someone held me down. He put clamps on my cut and sewed me up. It took a good hour to finish the job. I was very weak, and someone gave me some warm milk to drink. While he was working on me I began to think of my home in Poland before the war. It all rushed before my eyes during that hour. I was sad and sick at the same time.

After he finished, he told me to come back the next day. I went outside, sat on the bench again, and fainted right away. The doctor gave me something to smell and put a wet towel on my face. After a few minutes, I began to feel better. He asked me how far I had to walk home, and I told him I had to go to the slaughterhouse. It was a long way for a sick man to walk.

I talked to the doctor for a while and told him I was from White Russia, and my family was lost in the war. He listened to me and later found a woman to walk with me back to the slaughterhouse. I stayed in the room of the slaughterhouse near the stove and tried to rest. After a few days, I managed to get a place to sleep in the office, where it was warmer. My job was to start the fire in the morning before the workers came in. The room was still cold, but it was better than my other room. After a few weeks, my hand began to feel better. I still couldn't work in the slaughterhouse, but I managed to steal some fat and sell it for one hundred rubles. That wasn't a lot of money—a loaf of bread cost seventy rubles—but at least it was something.

I met a man who worked for a bakery, and he told me they needed an extra man. I went with him, but the man in charge didn't want me because I had a bad hand. I had to go back to the slaughterhouse. They weren't happy to have me return because I wasn't that much use to them with my hand. It was now the middle of the winter, and business was slow, so they sent me away.

※ ※

I went in a wagon with a few other men to a collective that was associated with the slaughterhouse. One night, after a meal of cooked potatoes, I went into a horse-drawn sled with the other men and traveled to the collective. At first I didn't know where I was going. The cold was intense. It was just like Siberia. We left at three in the afternoon and rode until twelve at night. I was frozen after that trip. It was not possible to stay warm, and we all suffered from the cold.

I went to work with the local blacksmith at the collective and stayed with him at his house. The blacksmith stayed with a local village girl and her child. Her husband was in the army, and she didn't even know if he was still alive. She had not seen him since the beginning of the war. Many men were drafted into the army, and their families never saw or heard from them for the entire war. The Russian Army did not give much importance to army men writing to their families. In any case, it was difficult to send letters in wartime.

The snow at the collective was so thick that it was impossible to see three feet in front of your face. It was easy to get lost and freeze to death. When we went to work in the morning, we had to tie a rope around our bodies and walk in a group. The snow was always several feet deep.

There was a Polish Jewish family living at the collective. The family consisted of one woman and her three girls. They were evacuated from Eastern Russia after the start of the war and came to the collective at that time. The husband and son were in the army and had not been heard from since the start of the war. They had a nice little house. Their job in the collective was to walk after the horses and pick up the droppings, which were used for fertilizer.

There was also a Rumanian girl in the collective with her little boy. Her husband was Polish and was in the Russian Army. She was a nice girl, and her stomach was bloated from hunger. She had to work all day and was very weak from the lack of food. She lived with the Jewish family. Later, when I could, I sent her a package of food. Her husband had been killed in the war, and the Jewish family was afraid to tell her. They shared their food with her, but it was not enough. That was a real tragedy. I felt terrible when I saw her. I wanted to help her, but there was not much I could do for her.

My time in the collective passed, and soon it was spring again. On May 14, 1945, we heard that the war was over. Germany was destroyed. All the people in the collective were running around singing. I was working on a horse and wagon when I heard the news. I had no feeling at all about the end of the war. I had lost everything in the war. I had no idea what was going to happen to me now that the war was over. I knew my family was dead. They were all killed by the Germans. I was sure of it. I didn't want to stay in Russia, but I had no idea what I wanted to do. I just had no emotions after hearing that the war was over.

I worked on that collective until the end of May 1945. The blacksmith borrowed one hundred fifty rubles from me at that time. I was staying with him, and I couldn't really say no to him. One day he told me there was no more work for me to do. I had to go see the director of the collective for more work. He told me to report to the local draft station. It was a beautiful spring day when I left. I walked there beside a wagon carrying wheat from the collective. I had to leave right away and never did get my money back from the blacksmith. I asked him for it, but he knew I was leaving and refused to give it to me. There was nothing I could do about it.

I reported to the draft station and waited. After a few days, a soldier came in and told me I was going back to Eulenburg. I didn't know what the army was going to do with me. The war was now over, and there was no danger from the fighting. But they might arrest me and put me back in a camp. I hoped I would not be in trouble because I was working and had legal papers. I had worked for the entire winter with the blacksmith. I had to wait for four more days at the draft station before the soldiers came for me. I lived on some old bread I had taken from the collective and some coffee I managed to buy. Finally a jeep came for me and two other men. We were taken to another collective some twelve kilometers away and had to wait in the manager's office. We were glad to get there and rest for a while. The jeep was always getting stuck in the mud, and we had to push it all the time. We were all tired from the trip.

The manager told us we were going to work on the collective for the time being. The land needed to be planted, and they needed a lot of help. The two other men with me were happy. They thought they would be able to steal a lot of food from the collective and would have an easy life. They later learned differently.

My work on the collective was to follow a tractor, cleaning its rake. It was a difficult job and physically very hard to do. The tractor pulled a large rake to prepare the land. I had to follow behind the rake and pick it up and remove anything that became stuck in the metal teeth. I was exhausted by the end of the day. I knew I wouldn't last long on that job and had to find some way to get out of it. The tractor driver was always in a hurry. He was paid by the amount of land he prepared and was always in a hurry. That was good for him but bad for me. I was paid nothing and saw no reason to work hard and kill myself for the collective.

I decided to walk slowly and do a bad job. The next day the tractor driver began to hurry, but I walked slowly and complained about my back and feet. The tractor driver became very angry at me and began to curse. I didn't listen to him and just walked slowly. At the end of the day he complained to the manager of the collective and said he wanted another man. I was happy to get out of that job.

The manager of the collective gave me another chance and told me I was to watch the goats at night. That was a good job to have. I could sleep during the day and rest at night while I watched the goats. That was the best job I had the entire time I was in Russia. I even milked the goats at night and had extra food. I took half a glass from every animal. I put some of the milk on the roof of my room, and after a few days had sour cream. I began to eat more and feel better.

By the middle of July a Russian lieutenant came to the collective and took me away. I had five minutes to pack and leave. They gave me no time to get ready. He told me I was going to be sent to the forest to cut wood. The army gave me extra food and money for the work, as well as a shirt and pair of pants. I had food for a month. I liked everything about the job except the cutting of the wood. That was hard work, and I didn't want any part of it. I went to the lieutenant and told him I didn't want to cut wood. I said I was sick and was in no condition for hard physical labor. He yelled at me and threatened to throw me in jail for shirking my duty. I just said I was a sick man and couldn't do that hard work. Many of the other men who were on the work detail ran away after they received their rations. I could have done the same, but I was tired of running and just decided to stay and take my chances. I sat around for a whole week and waited for orders. I had some money and could buy extra food when I needed it. I once saw one of the men who ran away at the food market, but I didn't talk to him.

A few days later, the lieutenant asked me if I would work in a warehouse. I agreed and worked in that warehouse until I left Russia. Every store in the town had to buy from the warehouse, and I could steal what I wanted.

A few months later, I was drafted from the warehouse to work on a sewer. I had to work on it for five days. I was working in a deep hole digging one night when I saw a nice-looking Jewish man praying. I began to talk to him. I told him my story, and we had a nice conversation in Jewish [Yiddish]. He invited me to come to his house, and he told me he had a niece who was in bad shape. Her parents were dead, and she visited him every Sunday. That was how I met my wife. She was nineteen at the time.

I began to sleep in the backyard of the uncle. They cleaned me up and made me take a bath twice a week. They cleaned my clothes for me, because they were afraid of my lice. After a few days, I began to think about my home in Poland. I couldn't get it off my mind. I knew my whole family was dead, and I cried. The uncle comforted me. I felt better after a while.

Chapter Twelve

I Leave Russia

I knew my wife for one month before I married her. I had to bribe my wife's boss with food so he would give her time off from work to get married. He was a big man in Russia and had an important job with the government. Still, there were many things he couldn't get and I could. I spent time buying and selling on the black market and could find almost anything I needed. I found out what he wanted and got it for him. He was happy, and my wife had a few days off from work to get married.

After we were married, we decided to leave Russia. There was no future there for us. We both worked and made money, but we couldn't spend it on anything we wanted. There was just nothing to buy. I could leave Russia because I was a Polish citizen, and the government was letting Poles go home after the war. My wife could get out because she was married to me. Only foreign citizens could leave. I had no desire to go back to my home village. With the change of borders after the war, my home village was now in Russia, and I wanted to leave Russia and Communism. I had had enough of them. In any case, there was no easy means of transportation to my village and conditions were still very dangerous.

I had some letters from people who returned to the village, and they told me that my entire family was dead. They were all killed by the Germans in the war. Many of the farmers stole things from the Jews and didn't want to see any Jews return. It was very dangerous for a Jew to return to that village. Some Jews who returned after the war were killed for asking too many questions. I have a friend from New York who went there in 1958 and stayed for one night. He was afraid to stay any longer. Even then, after so many years, the people didn't want to see any Jews return. He told me about the village and took some pictures. I could write a letter to some of the people I knew before the war, but what use would it be? I will never go back.

My wife and I left Russia in May 1946. We rode on a cargo train full of refugees returning to Poland. The Russians told us to be careful on the train since we were going to pass through the Ukraine. Many people there would shoot at the train if they knew Jews were on it. They really hated Jews in the Ukraine and were worse than the Germans.

When the train stopped, I saw large chunks of salt on the platform. I ran off the train and began to steal the salt. I loaded it on the car under the bunks. Everyone on the train was afraid to steal the salt. It belonged to the government, and I would be in trouble if I was caught, but I decided to take the chance. I knew I could sell it later for money and food, which I needed. I loaded so much salt on the car that other passengers told me they could see sparks flying from the wheels when we went around curves due to the excess weight. I took a chance and got away with it. Everyone on the train had something illegal. You couldn't take anything of value out of Russia except a few paper rubles, which were worthless once you crossed the border. Everyone had something of value that they were trying to smuggle out of the country. Some people had gold and jewelry. Many people had Russian gold rubles that were minted in the time of the Tsars.

When we arrived at the border, the Russian police checked us and took everything from us. They were looking for gold, but we did not have any. My wife had Russian government bonds which she was forced to buy during the war. The police took the bonds and all of our papers. They even took our marriage license. To this day there is no legal proof that we are married.

The police also took many people off the train. There were two brothers on the train. One of the brothers had married a Russian girl. He was traveling with his wife and her parents and his wife's sister. The police took the parents and sister off the train. The scenes were terrible. The people had to decide if they wanted to be split up or return to Russia. They had to make a terrible decision. There was no future for them in Russia, and they had sold all of their possessions. Many people were split from their families and never saw them again.

I started a fire on the train to cook food. We were on that train for a whole month and had no chance to buy hot food. It was impossible to build a fire at a station because we never knew how long the train was going to stay in the station. I kept a fire going in the car and had hot food. Many people in the car were nervous about my fire, but I was careful. We had metal pails and put potatoes and eggs in the pails to cook. At a few stops, people would come to the train to sell food. I traded my salt for food and anything else of value. There was no salt in many parts of Russia, and I could trade it for a lot of food. By the time the train got to Poland, I had a lot of food and money.

When we crossed into Poland, the train went from Lublin to the city of Krakow and then to a small city that was located on former German territory. When we got off the train, I thought I was going to stay in Poland for good. I knew nothing about Poland after the war. We went into a large camp for refugees and waited. I had to think about our future. We had no money, no family, and no friends.

⚞ ⚟

While we were in that camp, I saw something that made my heart break. I knew what the Germans were like and what they had done to the Jews during the war, and I still felt bad. Most of the people who lived in the houses were Germans. They stayed on in the area after the end of the war and were now being kicked out of their homes by the Poles. I saw a refugee go with a Polish policeman into a German house and tell the Germans he wanted their home, and they had two hours to pack and leave. The German couple didn't know what to do first. The man was shaving and began to run around the house. He didn't know if he should finish shaving or grab his belongings. It was a pitiful sight to see. There was a great feeling of hatred towards the Germans, and they had to leave. The man and his wife began to grab whatever they could. The wife grabbed a pair of pillows and ran down the street screaming. The man was in a state of shock. He just couldn't believe he was going to lose his home. That was how they forced the Germans to leave.

⚞ ⚟

After we arrived in Poland, I found a man from Lvov in Russia whom I knew during the war. I helped him out in Russia with some food, and he said he would smuggle my wife and me across the border to Czechoslovakia. He was making his living smuggling people, but he was going to help us for free. We had to make our decision soon because the Polish police were becoming suspicious of him, and he was planning to flee soon.

My problem was that my brother and cousin were still in Russia, and I didn't want to lose contact with them. I wrote them a letter soon after I arrived in Poland but had no reply. I told my friend I couldn't go with him across the border because I had to wait for my brother and cousin. He left a few days later, and I never saw him again.

The Hagana[9] was operating a kibbutz [collective community] in Poland for Jewish refugees, and we decided to go into the kibbutz. The real purpose of the kibbutz was to smuggle Jews out of Poland and into Palestine. I also wanted to be in the kibbutz for safety. There were many anti-Jewish riots in Poland, and it was dangerous for a Jew to be on the streets alone. In 1946, the Poles killed forty-eight Jews in the middle of the day in a pogrom. I didn't survive the war with the Germans and Russians to be killed in Poland in a pogrom. The Hagana had guns, and I knew I would be safe there. The Hagana wanted to take in only young people with no children or old parents. They needed young, healthy people to survive the trip over the border and then fight in Palestine. They knew my wife was pregnant at the time, but I persuaded them to take us anyway.

---

9   Editor's Note: The Hagana was a Jewish paramilitary organization that later became the Israeli Defense Forces.

While I was in the kibbutz, my wife and I had to ride a train. I was sitting on one bench, and my wife was sitting on another bench. In front of my wife were two men who were bragging about how many Jews they had killed during the war. They said they had pulled a religious Jew across a wooden sawhorse and sawed him in half alive. They described his screaming as his guts fell out and how they were all covered with his blood. They were very proud of their work and said they were sorry they couldn't kill more Jews. My wife and I just kept our heads down and said nothing. What the Germans started in Poland in 1939 many Poles wanted to finish in 1946.

My wife and I stayed in the kibbutz for three months before we got word that we were to leave for Czechoslovakia. My wife was advanced in her pregnancy, and I was worried that she couldn't walk the distance. Just before I was about to leave Poland, I got word that my brother was coming out of Russia. I had to wait for him. The kibbutz didn't want me to wait for my brother but said they would send him out later. I refused to go and had a big fight with the people in the kibbutz. I managed to stay in the kibbutz and wait for my brother.

After my brother arrived, we were ready to leave. My wife was very close to the end of her pregnancy. The kibbutz wanted my brother to stay and work for the kibbutz, but since my wife was close to having her baby, they had to let him go with us. They were not prepared for any babies at that kibbutz, and I refused to leave without my brother. We were allowed to carry two bags and one bag on our backs. Everyone had to carry his own bag. I couldn't carry anything for my wife. She had to carry her own bags. They didn't want me to get tired on the trip and not make the border by morning.

We walked in the dark through the cold woods for the better part of the night. The guards stopped us in Czechoslovakia and checked us for gold and silver. The Czech guards were very nice to us and gave us coffee and bread to eat. They put us on a train for a refugee camp in Vienna. My wife was uncomfortable and could not walk very well, but she covered the distance to the border with everyone else. We were both tired by the time the train arrived in Vienna. When we arrived at the refugee camp, I found a cot for my wife and told her to rest. I walked away to find some food, and my wife told me that a woman came over to her and threw her off the cot and took it for her daughter. That was how people were in the camps. They had suffered so much in the war; they just grabbed everything they could. They could think only of their own needs and took whatever they could.

After we had something to eat, we felt better. I was very tired and went right to sleep. I remember just before I fell asleep, I heard a woman crying. My wife told me later that the woman went into the shower and took off her girdle, which contained her money. The girdle was stolen while she was in the shower, and she lost everything. She was hysterical about the loss. That sort of thing happened all the time. You had to be very careful about your possessions in the camps.

After a few days, the authorities moved us to another camp at Nebenlager Bretstein, which was a former concentration camp. They had ovens there with tall chimneys. We were there for six weeks. Many people who were single and had no children left for Palestine at that time.

One day while my wife was at the doctor's for a check-up, she heard people running and yelling in the camp. There were thousands of people in the camp, and they were all running and screaming. I later found out what the problem was. During the war, there was a Jewish family that dug a tunnel from the camp to the outside and lived in a hole near the camp. They were afraid to go too far from the camp because they were Polish Jews, and the people around the camp were Austrian Germans, so they would be found out right away. They had to stay close to the camp to survive. They stayed near the camp, and their little girl would go back into the camp every few days to find some food and water. There were Jewish police in the camp who ran the camp for the Germans. The Germans would tell the Jewish police that they needed forty Jewish children to burn that day, and the Jewish police had to provide the children. The Jewish police would go to the barracks and choose the children. Sometimes if the parents had money, they could bribe the Jewish police to take another child. The police were always looking for those children in the camp to give to the Germans to kill. One Jewish policeman tried to grab the little girl, but she managed to get away from him and get back to her parents outside of the camp. She was terrified by the incident and would not return to the camp.

After the war, the camp became a refugee camp, and the Polish Jewish family returned to the camp to live. That day the girl was walking in the camp and saw the Jewish policeman who had tried to grab her and ran to her parents to tell them. Her parents told other people, and soon a mob of former camp inmates were chasing the man. Many had lost children and family in the camp, and they blamed him. They tried to kill him. They caught him near the fence and beat and kicked him. They knocked out one of his eyes and broke several ribs. American soldiers ran into the camp and saved his life. He was badly hurt, and I am sure he was a cripple for the rest of his life.

⛰ ⛰

After six weeks, we left that camp and went to another camp. There were many other refugees there in addition to the Jews. My daughter was born there on January 9, 1947.

Many of the Jewish women in the camp were suspicious of the camp hospital, which was staffed by Ukrainians and in which many Jewish babies died soon after birth. I took my wife to the local German hospital to have her baby. We were scared of the Germans, but trusted them more than the Ukrainians.

It was very cold when I brought my wife and daughter home from the hospital. We had a real procedure when we had to change the baby. The room we were in was cold, and I had to put the diaper on my chest to warm it before we put it on the baby. I then put a blanket over the baby and blew hot air into it to warm her. Then we put the baby under the blanket and changed her. We had to wrap her tight with many strings to keep her warm. We tried to be very careful with the baby, but even so, she was sick for many months with pneumonia, and we almost lost her during that first year.

Chapter Thirteen

Austria

When my wife returned from the hospital, there were some empty beds in the barracks and some extra blankets. I used to smuggle blankets out of the camp to sell to the Austrians. The tailors used the cloth to make clothes for the Germans. They had nothing after the war and would buy any piece of clothing. Every bed had two blankets, and since many people were passing through the camps, blankets were always missing. The authorities thought the people who passed through the camps were stealing them. Some did steal the blankets, but I stole many for myself. Everyone in the camp was cheating to survive. The people in the camp had been deprived for so long that they took everything they could. It was a way of life with the people in the camps.

I put two beds together for my wife and daughter and gave them some extra blankets. I found an old milk can and cut it in half for the baby. The ventilation was very poor in the barracks, and soon our area of the barracks began to smell. I opened the windows whenever I could to air out the barracks. Some people complained, but most were understanding. It was not easy to take care of a small baby in that building. We were cold and uncomfortable all the time and decided that we had to find another place to live.

I searched for another camp and soon found a better one that was located eighteen kilometers from us. It was a former German SS camp and was well built with strong brick buildings. My brother was with me at that time, and he had a job there working in the camp kitchen and told me about it. I moved my family there, and soon we were settled into our new home. We were no longer living in a large barracks but had our own individual rooms. It was wonderful compared to the last camp.

All of our food and clothing came from America. We sold some of the clothing to the Germans for fresh food. We had powdered milk and canned food from America and needed fresh food. We had to buy and sell on the black market to survive. All food and clothing was strictly regulated by the government with official stamps, and we had no ration stamps. There were about four thousand people in the camp, and they all bought and sold on the black market when needed.

In 1947, I became involved in supplying kosher meat to the people in the camp. There was a ritual slaughterer in the camp, and he would work for me. I would go to the Austrian farmers and buy cows to slaughter for the camp. We had no other way of getting fresh meat. I could carry a small animal back in two trips from the farmer, but a larger animal had to be brought right into the camp to be slaughtered. There were some loose boards in the rear of the fence, and I would bring the cattle right through the fence. I started slowly at first, but soon I was supplying meat to most of the people in the camp.

The farmers were not supposed to sell us cattle. They had to sell all their cattle to the government for the official price, but they needed the money and were willing to take a chance with me. I sold the excess non-kosher meat to the local Austrian butchers for a good price. I still gave it to them for a lot cheaper than they could buy from the government. Everyone was happy and made money. I had to be very careful because the Austrian police were constantly checking people from the camp who they suspected of dealing with the black market.

I was stopped by the police a few times, but was always very lucky. I was also very careful and planned my operations with great care. After a while, the police began to suspect me and began to watch me carefully. The police were very careful how they handled the Jews. They knew the Jews had suffered much in the war and were always very polite to us. I felt I had nothing to worry about as far as they were concerned.

One day I was driving back to the camp on my bicycle with a load of meat when the police tried to stop me. I remember the policeman yelling at me, "Stehenbleiben, stehenbleiben!" He wanted me to stop, but since I was not too far from the camp, I decided to make a run for it. I knew I would be safe once I got into the camp. The Austrian police never came into the camp. They had no authority there. It was no use. Before I could get away, another policeman grabbed me. I was caught with a load of illegal meat. I had to walk with them to the police station. I heard them saying in German that I might try to run, but I decided against it. They were watching me too carefully, so I had to go with them.

The police put me in a cell for the night. The next morning they began to question me about my meat. I told them I left the camp to buy some fresh meat for my family from a man I had recently met, and that was all I knew. I was just buying some fresh meat for my family. They didn't believe me and wanted to know the name of the farmer I was dealing with. I refused to tell them, because I wanted to protect the farmer. He would be in serious trouble with the government if he was caught dealing with the black market. I knew I was a refugee, and they couldn't really hurt me. I also had half a cow waiting for me in the farmer's cellar, and I didn't want to lose that meat.

They told me I was under arrest and put handcuffs on me and made me walk through the center of the town to another station. Everyone in the town could see me, and many people from the camp saw me also. Later that day, my brother came to see me and brought me some bread and milk. Shortly after my brother left, the police decided to let me go. I refused to talk, and they really couldn't do anything with me. Soon after I was released, I took my bicycle and returned to the farmer to pick up the rest of the meat. I waited a week in the camp, and then decided to go back into business. I just became tired of sitting in the camp. I also had a down payment on a cow and didn't want to lose it.

I now formed a company in the camp to sell beef. I got ten men together, and each man put in five hundred shillings to finance the company. I would take the money and go to the farmers to buy the cattle. Then I would bring the cattle back to the camp to slaughter. There were many different companies of butchers in the camp, and people were always going from one company to another to work and invest their money. My brother worked with me and acted as my banker and kept the money for me. I put a false bottom on the baby carriage, and my wife would make some of the meat deliveries for me. She would take the baby for a walk and drop the meat off at the local butcher shop. I used to bring the cattle right into the barracks to slaughter them. Once I bought a steer that was so big that he fell right through the floor of the barracks. The ritual slaughterer would come into the barracks, and the rabbi would check to see that everything was kosher.

I also sold fresh meat to the local hotels. Once I was in the kitchen of a local hotel when I noticed that something was wrong. The owner of the hotel told me not to worry and went on looking at the meat I brought him. Just then a man in the kitchen announced that he was from the police and told everyone to stay put. I jumped up and ran out the front door through the main dining room. I got outside and jumped over a fence and ran to the railroad station. The police ran after me, but I blended in with the crowd and was soon lost. When I saw them start checking the papers of people in the station, I slipped out the other end and ran back to the barracks. I had to send my wife back to the hotel the next day to get my bicycle. I was very happy to get away from the police and stayed out of trouble for a few days. I didn't want to go to jail again. After a while I became tired of staying in the camp and went back to work again.

I decided that my work would be safer if I had a better form of transportation. I got rid of my bicycle and bought a German Army motorcycle. The wheels were the size of jeep wheels, and it could go anywhere. I bought it from a German SS man and had to send it to Salzburg for three months to be repaired. When it came back from Salzburg, it was in top condition.

⚔ ⚔

Many people in the camp wanted to go to America. I wanted to go to America, but I needed a sponsor. I had some relatives in America, but they were not willing to sponsor me. They told me to go to Israel. I could go to Israel anytime and was having a good time in the camp, so I decided to wait for my chance to go to America.

Soon after I registered to go to America, I received word from my brother-in-law that he was coming from Poland through Austria on a train on his way to Israel. I had not seen him since the war started and was anxious to see him again. I knew the train schedule and where it would pass through the American zone of Austria. My brother-in-law had spent the war in the woods with the partisans. After the war, he was in the Polish Army and could get out legally by going to Israel. I took my motor-cycle and a package of food and drove to the train station to wait for him. I went with another man from the camp who wanted to see his sister, who was on the train. His sister wrote him and told him she wanted to jump off the train to be with him. Many people tried to jump off the refugee trains from Poland and get into the camps. Once in the camps, they had a chance to get to America or England. Life was very hard in Israel at that time, and many people didn't want to go there. They had suffered in the war and wanted a better life in America.

The Austrian police knew that the refugees wanted to get off the train, so they surrounded the train whenever it stopped. They grabbed many people who jumped off and put them back on the train. When the train came to the station, I saw my brother-in-law and jumped into the train through an open window. The police ran to the window and ordered me off the train. I refused and stayed there with him for two hours while the train was at the station. He told me he wanted to get off, and I urged him to jump. I told him I had my motorcycle with me, and the police would never catch us. He was afraid to take the chance and stayed on the train and went to Israel. I jumped off the train when it left the station and followed it on my bike to the next station where I jumped back onto the train again. We had a lot to talk about after so many years.

After the train pulled out of the station, I heard two voices calling, "Help! Help!" The police had already left, and I was the only one there. I saw two men hiding behind a pile of bricks. They had jumped off the train and wanted to get to a refugee camp. This was their second escape attempt. The first time they were found by the police and put back on the train. They had no papers and had to avoid the police. They were both dressed lightly, and it was a cold and rainy night. I took them on my motorcycle back to the camp. I had a sidecar on the motorcycle and one man laid down on the floor of the car while the other sat up.

I started home on the back roads to stay away from the police. I was going very fast and found it difficult to see. I went only a short distance when the front wheel hit some loose blocks on the road and the whole bike turned over. No one was hurt, but the front light on the bike was broken. Now I had no light and couldn't even see a few feet in front of me. We were on the back roads, and there was no light of any type. It was too dark to drive, and I had to stop for the night.

We found a small village and decided to sleep just outside of the village. I pulled the bike off the road and went to sleep under a tree. We were there for about an hour when a policeman woke us up. Since I was the only one who knew German, I talked to him. I had my papers and showed them to him and told him we were on our way back to the camp. The other two men stayed behind me and never said a word. The policeman looked at my papers and didn't check my companions. After he left, we decided to leave the area in case he came back. We slept in the woods for the night. When it was light enough to see, we drove back to the camp. Once in the camp, they were safe. They got a set of papers and could go anywhere.

One month later, a man came to see me with a proposition. He wanted me to smuggle other Jews off the refugee trains into the camps. He offered me a lot of money, but I decided it was too dangerous. I had a good business selling meat and didn't want to take any more chances. The two men I brought back gave him a good report, and I was famous all over the camp. They thought I could do anything. I decided to stay away from that business. I wanted to go to America and knew I would never have a chance if I had a record with the police. I did many things in the camps that were not legal, but moving people seemed too dangerous. I stayed away from the smuggling business.

⊿ ⊾

I had no sponsor to come to America, so I had to wait over five years in that camp in Austria. Finally, in 1950, the HIAS organization [Hebrew Immigrant Aid Society] agreed to help me come to this country. I was very happy when I heard I was leaving Austria for America. I knew nothing about America and couldn't even speak English, but I was hopeful about my future. I had had a difficult time in Europe and had suffered much. I had lost my home and family and everything that was important to me. Still I survived and was alive. I would do well in America. I arrived here in 1951 to begin my new life. I was a long way from my little village of Czuczewicze in Poland.

The Neiman Family in Czuczewicze

During the course of research for this book, the editors discovered that in 1969 Yitzkhak Neiman submitted "pages of testimony" about his family members who were killed in the Holocaust. These pages are now located online in the Central Database of Shoah Victims' Names maintained by Yad Vashem at db.yadvashem.org.

This appendix includes an image of the page Mr. Neiman submitted about his wife Lea,, and his twin sons, Yaakov and Aharon (or Avraham). The information in the Database also allowed us to construct a family tree for the members of the Neiman family who lived in Czuczewicze before the Second World War.

Figure 1. The Neiman family in Czuczewicze before World War II, based on Yitzkhak Neiman's submissions to the Central Database of Shoah Victims' Names. Mr. Neiman also had two brothers who are not listed in the Database. One of his brothers was killed while serving in the Russian Army during the war, and the other moved to Israel after the war. Both of these brothers appear in Mr. Neiman's narrative above.

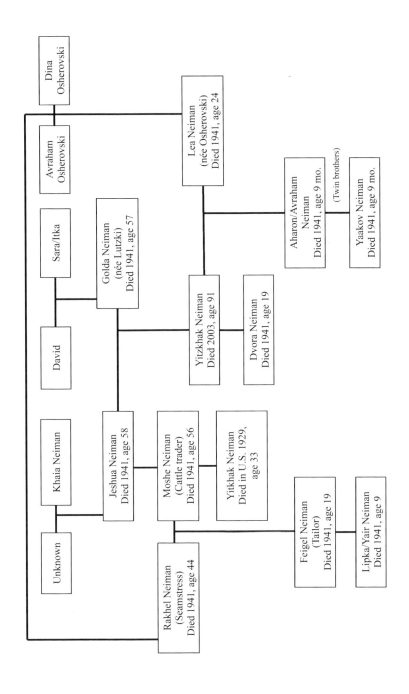

Figure 2. Mr. Neiman's page of testimony about his first wife, Lea Neiman (née Osherovsky) from the Central Database of Shoah Victims' Names. According to this page, Lea was 24 years old when she was executed by the Germans in 1941. Lea and Yitzkhak Neiman's twin sons, who were killed at 9 months old, are also listed on this page about Lea.

Dr. Harry A. Butowsky

Dr. Harry A. Butowsky retired on June 30, 2012, from the National Park Service in Washington D.C. where he worked as an historian and manager for the National Park Service History e-Library web site. Dr. Butowsky has served at an adjunct professor of history at George Mason University since 1980 where teaches History of World War I and World War II in Europe and World War II in the Pacific. His Ph.D. is from University of Illinois.

Dr. Butowsky is a regular contributor to National Parks Traveler, a web based magazine (http://www.nationalparkstraveler.com) and manages two web sites, npshistory.com and parkscanadahistory.com. Dr. Butowsky is also a frequent guest speaker for many public events in Northern Virginia, DC and Maryland.

ALSO BY DR. HARRY A. BUTOWSKY

Leopold von Ranke and the Jewish Question
University of Illinois, 1975

Appomattox Manor-City Point, A History
National Park Service 1978

Man in Space-National Historic Landmark Theme Study
National Park Service 1983

Warships Associated with World War II in the Pacific
National Park Service 1985

*The U.S. Constitution-A National Historic Landmark
Theme Study*
National Park Service 1988

*Astronomy and Astrophysics- A National Historic Landmark
Theme Study*
National Park Service 1989

Geology National Historic Landmark Theme Study
National Park Service 1990

An American Family in World War II
Sandra O'Connell, Ralph L. Minker and
Harry Butowsky
Word Association Publishers 2005

Acknowledgements

This book would never have been completed without the support and encouragement of the following people:

I would like to first thank my wife, Lois Butowsky, who accompanied me in many visits with Mr. Neiman, his wife, daughter, and grandson in 1974. Lois also encouraged me to record Mr. Neiman's story. After I retired from the National Park Service in 2012 she never failed to remind me that I had an unfinished manuscript sitting on my bookshelf and that I should complete this history. I also want to thank my daughter, Karen Butowsky, who found the original tapes I used to record Mr. Neiman's story. She encouraged me to buy a new tape machine to listen to the material. Once I did so I realized that I had captured most of his story with great accuracy. I also realized that I needed to make many updates regarding proper and place names.

Dr. Beverly Blois from Northern Virginia Community College looked at the manuscript and urged me to finish it. Dr. Ralph Ostrich, Reene Newton, Dr. David Fuchs, and his wife Benita also read the manuscript and sent suggestions and useful maps to illustrate the story. I had many talks with my good friends Barbara and Morton Libarkin about the manuscript. Barbara Libarkin helped me with the many Yiddish terms Mr. Neiman used to describe his experiences.

I would also like to thank my students at George Mason University, who listened to me read portions of Mr. Neiman's story in my class and asked questions and offered suggestions. I also owe special gratitude to one young lady who showed me the proper spelling of Czuczewicze and located it on a map using her cell phone while I was giving my lecture. I remain amazed at the power of technology after this incident.

I also owe a debt to my publisher, Tom Costello from Word Association Publishers, for reading the manuscript and encouraging me to finish it. Tom assigned Dr. Heather Steffen as my editor. She improved the writing and greatly contributed to the quality of the final product. I found Dr. Steffen to be a first-class editor and historian, and I came to rely on her suggestions more and more as the history neared completion.

Finally, I need to thank Mr. Isadore (Yitzkhak) Neiman, who spent many hours with me 1974 and 1975 telling me his very personal story. This was not easy for him, and I believe this was the first and only time Mr.

Neiman related his entire story to anyone since he came to America in 1951.

No history is complete or fully accurate. Any mistakes are my own, but I did record Mr. Neiman's story as he told it to me.

Harry Butowsky,
August 20, 2015
Reston, Virginia

WA